50p

HEADLINE HISTORY

The Nineteenth Century

John Ray

GW00641762

Evans Brothers Limited

Published by Evans Brothers Ltd
Montague House, Russell Square,
London WC1B SBX

Filmset by BAS Printers Limited,
Over Wallop, Hampshire

Printed and bound in Great Britain by
The Garden City Press Limited, Letchworth, Hertfordshire SG6 1JS

First published by J. M. Dent and Sons Ltd 1973
New edition published by Evans Brothers Ltd 1978

ISBN 0 237 29211 4   PRA 5749

Contents

Acknowledgments

The author and publishers would like to thank
the following for their permission to reproduce
photographs:

Hull Museums: p. 29

Mansell Collection: pp. 6, 7, 8, 9, 10, 14, 16, 17,
18, 19, 20, 21, 22, 25, 28, 31, 32, 33, 34, 39, 42, 44,
46, 47, 49, 50, 51, 58, 65, 66, 68, 70, 71, 72, 75, 77, 80,
83, 85, 88, 91, 92, 93, 94, 96, 100, 105, 106, 107, 117,
119, 121, 123, 127

Montagu Motor Museum: p. 122

Radio Times Hulton Picture Library: pp. 5,
12, 15, 23, 24, 27, 30, 35, 36, 37, 38, 40, 43, 52, 53,
55, 56, 57, 59, 60, 62, 64, 67, 73, 76, 79, 82, 84, 86,
90, 98, 100, 101, 103, 104, 109, 110, 111, 112, 113, 115,
116, 118, 124, 125, 128

1805
Trafalgar

DEATH IN THE HOUR OF VICTORY

Great victory for our ships: The nation mourns Lord Nelson: Skill and daring win the day

When the ships were about one hundred and eighty metres apart, the firing started. Gun flashes spurted from their sides. Black smoke rolled by in clouds. Then came the hits. Cannon balls cut through sails and rigging. Spars were splintered and came crashing to the decks. A huge mast snapped at the base and toppled over. Shots smashed into the sides. Some ploughed through gun-ports, striking men and weapons. Plumes of water rose into the air as cannon-balls fell short.

Below decks, there was a terrible noise and confusion. The crews, stripped to the waist, heaved and pulled at their guns. They dragged them into fresh positions. It was impossible to hear commands, so the master-gunners had to make hand-signals to their men. As the enemy shot came crashing in, ropes, woodwork and guns were shattered. Pieces were hurled about. Men fell, dead or wounded. Some, with shattered limbs, were carried below. Bodies were pushed out of the way so that the fight could be continued. Sailors moved in a daze, so great was the din, the smoke and the confusion. In some places the decks ran with blood and the living could hardly keep their feet as the ship pitched. In between salvoes, cheers, screams and groans could be heard.

The date was 21st October 1805 and one of the greatest actions in the whole of naval history was being fought. It was the Battle of Trafalgar, which has become one of the most famous events in Britain's naval story. Cape Trafalgar is a headland on the south-western coast of Spain. On that day, a fleet of the Royal Navy met a combined French and Spanish fleet. The action which followed was of great importance for both sides.

Wars between Britain and France lasted, with almost no break, between 1793 and 1815. From 1803 the French Emperor, Napoleon, had developed a number of ideas for defeating his British enemies. He wished to land an army in England. His military power was so great that if he had succeeded in landing a strong body of

Nelson in deep thought before the battle

5

The battle at its height

troops on English soil, they might well have conquered the country.

However, England could be attacked only by sea. It was necessary first of all to gain control of part of the English Channel. Napoleon hoped to draw together large units of his fleet. Then he could keep English ships away while his soldiers were transported. Many landing barges were made ready in Boulogne and nearby ports. If he could command the Channel for a few days only, that would be sufficient to move his famous army by sea.

But Napoleon knew little about naval warfare. He did not realise how tides and winds could make an enormous difference to sea fighting. It was not simply a matter of ordering a squadron of vessels to appear in a certain place at a given time. A great deal depended upon weather conditions which could change suddenly.

Britain relied upon her 'wooden walls'. As a seafaring, trading nation, the Royal Navy was of supreme importance to the country's defence. The ships were used to stop French overseas trade. Also, they lay outside French ports for long periods. Sometimes they waited for the enemy to come out and fight. At other times they blockaded the French vessels in their own harbours.

Admiral Lord Nelson was the British commander in the Mediterranean. He had already gained the reputation of being a superb sailor.

In previous actions he had lost an arm and an eye while fighting brilliantly. His tasks were to protect British ships trading there and to keep a special watch on the French fleet in Toulon. By 1805, Napoleon realised that he must make a last effort to invade the shores of England. He wanted his ships to gather for the attempt. The fleet at Toulon sailed out under the command of Admiral Villeneuve on the 30th March. Nelson's ships followed in pursuit. The chase went to the West Indies, where Napoleon had hoped to gather his fleet before the invasion attempt was made. By moving towards the wealthy West Indies, the French hoped to draw some of the heavily stretched British fleet away from the Channel.

By the late summer, however, the French plans were not working out. Villeneuve's fleet returned to Europe. Ideas of invading England were given up. Then he sailed south and entered the harbour at Cadiz, in Spain. The Spanish and French were allies. Their combined strength there amounted to thirty-three ships-of-the-line and seven frigates. Nelson, in pursuit, lay outside with twenty-seven ships-of-the-line and four frigates.

The ships under Villeneuve's command put out from Cadiz on the 20th October. Altogether they carried 2,626 guns. Nelson's vessels mounted 2,148 guns. On the next morning, the two fleets drew close off Cape Trafalgar.

Nelson had spent long hours planning his attack. He intended to destroy the enemy, not just drive them away. His second-in-command, Admiral Collingwood was to attack the rear of the enemy line, using fifteen ships. Nelson, with the remaining twelve vessels would close with the front of their force. The battle began about midday. Collingwood's attack on the rear of the Franco-Spanish fleet brought confusion. Nelson, in his flagship, H.M.S. *Victory* bore down with his ships on the front of the enemy's line. Then they closed in and began the close action.

The guns fired solid shot. They varied in size from the enormous 32-pounders, each of which weighed three and a half tons, to the small 6-pounders. Ships sailed in until they were sometimes only 20 or 30 metres apart. The effect of heavy fire at such close range was murderous. In this form, the main action went on for about four hours.

Nelson's brilliant tactics brought rapid results. Individual Spanish and French ships fought bravely. However, they were no match for the British attack. After receiving withering gunfire, a number of Villeneuve's vessels surrendered.

But the British success was soon dimmed. A number of snipers were positioned up in the rigging of some French vessels. One of them shot Nelson. The ball entered his shoulder as he walked on deck. It went down to lodge in his spine. He was carried below, but nothing could be done to save him. In the moment of victory, he died.

Villeneuve's fleet lost twenty vessels which were either captured or sunk. He himself surrendered. The British lost no ships but many men were killed or wounded. The victory proved that the French did not have the naval power to escort an invasion army to Britain. The newspapers soon reported the event. They showed a mixture of pride and sadness. A battle had been won, but the nation's best and most popular sailor had been lost.

Sea power played a crucial part in the Napoleonic Wars. British ships were able to protect the homeland. Also they stopped much of France's trade. In the long run, the Royal Navy played a vital part in defeating the French. For the rest of the century, Britain had the largest and most powerful fleet in the World.

On board the Victory *during the action*

1811
The Luddite Riots

WORKERS FEAR FOR THEIR JOBS

More machine breaking: Violence against factory owners: Government takes stern measures

The group of workmen were desperate. There were about a dozen of them and they were determined that no one should stand in their way. Keeping close together, they ran up the path towards the door of the small factory where some of them worked.

Although it was a dark night they could see a figure standing by the door. When they came closer, the man was recognised as the manager and owner. Hearing that the men were on the way, he had hurried to the factory, trying to stop them. Now he told them to go. He said that they had no right to be there. He intended to call the local magistrates and report them.

In reply, one of the group leapt forward. With his stick he hit the manager a blow on the side of the head. The victim reeled back and was then struck several times. He fell unconscious. The other men jumped over his body. They were carrying axes, sticks, sledgehammers and iron bars. One hefty man smashed at the door with an axe. It soon splintered and crashed open.

They dashed in eagerly. Two of the men were carrying small oil lamps. They now crouched to light them, using tinder boxes. After a few minutes, the lamps showed inside the factory. The gang knew where to look for the objects of their visit.

These were four new machines which stood apart from the rest of the machinery on the ground floor. They were stocking-frames and had been installed only a short time before. Quickly the men rushed up to them and began

their attack. Their eyes gleamed with savage hatred as they smashed at the machines. Axe and hammer blows crashed down on to the wood and metal. Chips of wood and pieces of iron flew up into the air. Blow after blow crashed down until the four machines had been utterly broken.

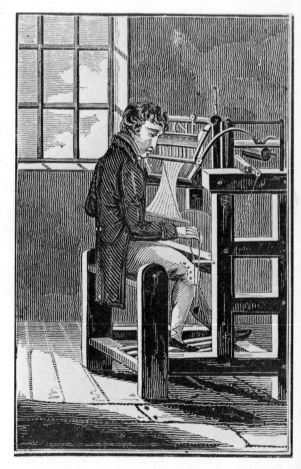

A weaver working at a stocking-frame

As the men stood back, panting with their efforts, a noise was heard outside. One of the group looked out of the door just as a group of constables and armed soldiers burst in. A fierce battle followed. Some of the gang were terrified and tried to run out. A few escaped. Others knew that surrender could mean death and fought madly. Suddenly a shot was fired and one of the workmen groaned as he pitched forward on to the floor. A musket-ball had smashed into his chest. This act caused the fighting to stop. The workmen surrendered. They dropped the tools of destruction which had been turned into weapons. The still flickering lamps showed their sullen faces as they were led away.

The year was 1811. When the incident described above happened, Britain was at war with France. The war had brought misfortune to workers in some areas. Those who were stocking-makers near Nottingham suffered particularly. They made their living from knitting stockings. Many of them were skilled craftsmen. Now, however, they feared for the future.

In the first place, the price of bread had risen sharply. Bread was their basic food. The French had stopped supplies of corn coming to Britain as part of their campaign. Therefore the British people had to rely on what they could grow for themselves. But the harvest of 1810 had been poor, and prices rose as a result.

Trade grew slack. There had been less demand for the work of stocking-makers than there had been a few years before. For generations they had produced stockings on frames in their own homes. At such a time the workers looked hard at anything which stood in the way of their earning a living wage. They especially hated the new machinery called stocking-frames.

These were pieces of machinery which could carry out work quickly. They produced at a faster rate than hand workers could. Therefore they appeared to be a threat. As times grew harder, some workers decided that the hated machines would have to be removed. If the factory owners would not agree to do away with them, then the workers would take the law into their own hands.

The shooting of a factory owner by the Luddites

The men called themselves Luddites. They claimed to be led by a mysterious figure known as 'King Ludd', or 'Ned Ludd'. It is not certain whether or not such a person existed. The Nottingham Luddites said that their leader lived in Sherwood Forest.

The authorities became very worried by the activities of the Luddites. Therefore they made the punishments more severe for anyone who was caught breaking machines. Already, a person could be transported for up to fourteen years if found guilty. They were sent to Australia. But now the government made the crime a capital offence. This meant that people could be hanged. Yet in spite of this harshness, the Luddites continued their work.

There were outbreaks of violence in other areas also. By 1812 it had spread to Lancashire, Cheshire and Yorkshire. Handloom machines and shearing machines were broken up. Workers there feared the new machinery which threatened their living. A shortage of food and the resulting high prices made them desperate. They gained great satisfaction from breaking the hated machines.

Machine breakers: from a series of drawings done in the 1830s

The violence grew. In Lancashire, a mill owner named Burton defended the looms in his factory. Five of the attacking Luddites were killed. In Yorkshire, a mill owner named Cartwright shot and killed two men who were attempting to break in. In April 1812 another owner, William Horsfall, was shot and killed by Luddites.

Spies were used by the authorities in an attempt to find details of the plots. These men joined groups of Luddites. In some cases, they tried to persuade men to cause trouble. Then they could be arrested.

A number of workers were hanged for taking part in attacks on machinery. Yet many were men who could think of no other way of protest against their conditions. The coming of machines and factories brought great benefits to most of the people of Britain. It was a period of invention known as the Industrial Revolution. However, it also brought suffering to some. They were the men who suddenly found that their skill was no longer required. Others found that machines could produce goods more rapidly than human beings could. The Luddites were a small, but important chapter in the story of the Industrial Revolution.

1812
The Retreat from Moscow

NAPOLEON'S FATAL MISTAKE

Huge French defeat: Napoleon's army in retreat; Fierce Russian pursuit

The villagers could hardly believe their eyes as the soldiers passed. Surely this was not the same army which had passed through their village just a few months before. Could this really be the Grand Army of the Emperor Napoleon which had gone to battle against Russia?

The date then had been May 1812. On a bright day they had turned out to watch units of the army go past. It had been a brilliant sight. Column after column of infantry had marched along. They were dressed in magnificent uniforms. One of their bands played and several of the soldiers sang. Then came lancers and hussars, jogging easily on their mounts. The harness jangled and lances glinted in the sunshine. Heavily plodding horses dragged guns along. At the rear came lines of carts carrying equipment of all kinds – ammunition, medical supplies, pontoon bridges and clothing. This was to be the army which would conquer Russia. It would sweep away all resistance. The Russians would be defeated and the Czar would be compelled to surrender to Napoleon.

But now the date was January 1813. The same villagers were watching the return of the soldiers. The weather was bitterly cold and the earth was deeply frozen, with snow and ice. Men trudged along wearily. Their uniforms were in tatters. Hands and feet were covered by lengths of shabby cloth. Some leaned on their comrades for support. Many had thrown away their weapons in an effort to keep going. Carts lurched past, carrying wounded men who had been packed on to the straw-covered floors. A number had frozen to death, but had not been removed. At the side of the column were horses, so underfed that their ribs showed clearly. It was an army of defeat and despair which passed by in silence.

Napoleon was one of the greatest figures who has ever appeared in history. In the early years of the nineteenth century, no enemy could match him as a military commander. His armies marched across Europe, defeating their opponents with some overwhelming victories. Austrian, Prussian and Russian armies were overthrown. The French Emperor was master of large areas of the continent.

In 1807, Napoleon signed a treaty with the Russian Czar, Alexander I. It was the Treaty of Tilsit. Each side agreed to offer some help to the other. A period of peace then began between the two nations. However, it was an uneasy peace. The two sides did not really trust each other. Gradually, events happened which ended the friendship.

One which caused especial argument was the Continental System. Napoleon tried to stop Britain's trade by not allowing her goods to be taken to any continental port. But the Russians discovered that this plan harmed their trade. Therefore, at the end of 1810 they passed a law which opened their ports to neutral ships. At the same time, they placed taxes on imported French goods.

There were other disagreements also. Gradually they led to a breakdown of relations between the two countries. Napoleon determined to launch a war against Russia. He decided that it would be a short campaign. His armies would strike with a few crushing blows. Then, when he had defeated the Russians, he would be able to give more attention to attacking his old enemy – Britain.

Thus it was that in 1812 Napoleon gathered together the Grand Army. Units moved eastward across Europe, towards the Russian frontier. The soldiers came from a number of countries. There were Austrians, Spaniards, Swiss and Prussians; there were Dutch, Italians, Poles and, of course, Frenchmen. By June, the Emperor had drawn up a massive army along the line of the River Niemen. It consisted of more than 500,000 men. They had more than 1,000 pieces of artillery with them and over 150,000 horses.

On 24th June this great force crossed the Niemen and the war began. The troops began the big drive towards the east. At first, as they moved through Russian Poland, many of the inhabitants were friendly. But as they entered Russia, the troops of the Grand Army found that the fighting grew harder.

The distances to be covered were vast. Roads were bad and the sun blazed down on the open plains. Napoleon hoped that the Russian armies would stand and fight. Then he would be able to give them a crushing defeat. However, they kept up a careful retreat. Their troops would not allow themselves to be cornered. Nevertheless, they inflicted heavy losses on Napoleon's men. By the time that they reached Smolensk, 540 kilometres inside the frontier, the French had lost almost 100,000 troops.

At length there was a pitched battle at Borodino on 7th September. The Russians retreated, but the invaders had suffered heavy losses. They pressed on towards Moscow, the Russian capital. Napoleon's forces entered the city on 14th September. They found that their enemy had deserted the place and set it on fire. Three-quarters of the city was destroyed. The French, who had come so far, had gained so little. The Russians merely retreated and laid waste to the country. They would not surrender.

Napoleon remained in Moscow for about five weeks, hoping that the Czar would seek peace. But the delay was fatal. His army had

The Emperor leads his retreating soldiers

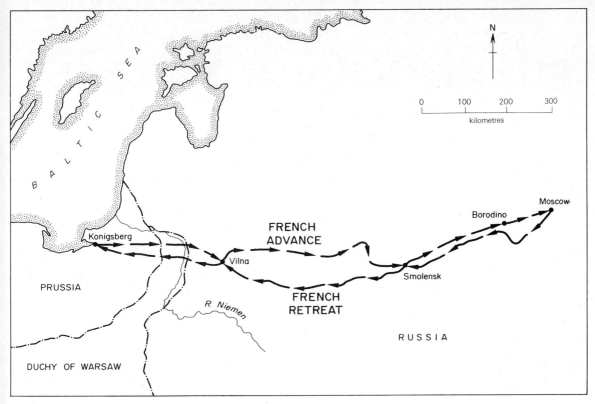

Napoleon's Russian campaign

lost spirit. Men and animals were desperate for food. He ordered a retreat on 19th October.

Thus began one of the most dreadful retreats ever. As his men struggled back towards the west, the Russians closed in to harry them. Regiments were isolated and cut to pieces. They could find supplies neither for themselves nor for their animals. The countryside was like a desert. The French marshal, Ney, fought well in rearguard actions, but he could not stop the fierce attacks.

The Russian winter set in. The cold was bitter. The invading army had never experienced such cruel weather. Men and beasts were frozen. Thousands died in the snow and blizzards.

On 27th November, the army crossed the River Beresina. Only their courage saved them from utter destruction as the Russians attacked the dejected troops. Soon afterwards, Napoleon left his men and returned to France, where trouble had been reported. The army was put under the command of Marshal Murat. At length the shattered remains of the Grand Army returned. They crossed the Prussian frontier during December and January. There they were watched by the amazed villagers who had seen them set out triumphantly just a few months before.

Napoleon's army had been shattered. About 200,000 men had perished. His enemies took heart from his defeat. They united again in another effort to overthrow him.

1813
Elizabeth Fry at Newgate

WOMEN'S CHAMPION ACTS

The plight of women and children in prison: Mrs Fry gives help: Should the Government do more?

She had heard of the conditions at the prison. Stories had been told for some time of how badly the women there were treated. But now she was able to see for herself just how they lived. What she saw was quite as bad as the worst stories that she had been told. It was hard to believe that human beings could exist in such circumstances.

Elizabeth Fry was a Quaker. She was a member of a strictly religious group which set high standards of service towards others. When she heard about the women in Newgate Prison, she became determined to go there.

Elizabeth Fry

They needed care and attention. As a Quaker, she felt a special love for her fellow men and women. Such people could not be left alone in their misery.

The year was 1813. She stood inside a large room at Newgate. The door behind her had just been closed and locked by the jailer. He was a worried man. In his view, it was madness for a lady to go in there. She would be harmed. At the least they might rob her. Some of them were quite capable of killing her. But he had to obey orders. He stood outside and listened, expecting to hear uproar.

Elizabeth Fry had asked to be allowed into the part of the prison where women were kept. She particularly wanted to meet the prisoners, face to face. Now she was there. Her great religious faith gave her confidence. But she realised that some of the women facing her were hardened criminals.

The scene was surprising. The room was filled with noisy, chattering women and their children. Clothing was littered everywhere, among pots, pans and people's belongings. In this room and another similar one were crowded about three hundred women and their many children. Almost all were dirty and unkempt. Some lay on the ground, shutting themselves off from the rest. Others screamed and shouted, laughing and quarrelling. Their children climbed over bundles of clothes, rolled and tumbled through groups of women. They were pushed, slapped and sworn at.

Elizabeth had another woman with her. She was a Quaker friend named Anna Buxton. The sight of the two women inside the prison cell soon brought attention from some of the prisoners. They gathered round. Mrs Fry had brought some small bundles of clothing.

Mrs Fry reads to the prisoners

Her kindness and calmness soon caught their interest. Here was somebody who was sparing time for them and their children. She was offering them help. They liked her.

It had not been easy for Elizabeth Fry and her friend to gain admission to the women's part of the prison. The governor was Mr Newman. He was unwilling to allow her to enter. Her request to go into the cells was most unusual. But at last he gave permission. Mrs Fry thus began the work for which she has become famous. Before the early nineteenth century, there had been few people interested in prisons and prisoners. The law was harsh and often savage. People who committed crimes were often punished severely.

In 1813, crime was a great problem in some parts of Britain. The coming of large industrial cities and towns brought many troubles. There was no official, organised police force. Some people found it easy to make a dishonest living. Others found the conditions of life so hard that they were forced to turn to crime.

During the later eighteenth century, the law had grown more severe. By 1800, there were about 200 offences which could be punished by death. This meant that the criminal was publicly hanged. Stealing was a crime which could bring the death penalty. Such savage punishments were intended to stop criminals from daring to commit crimes. Another common punishment was transportation. The criminal was taken by ship to one of the colonies. America was used until the 1770s. By the end of the century, Australia had convict settlements.

A few people in Britain were not satisfied with the amount of crime and the state of prisons. A famous pioneer who wanted reform was John Howard. In his writings he suggested that prisoners should be kept in clean conditions. They should be given work to do.

A prison hulk

Elizabeth Fry was born in 1780. She was the daughter of a rich Quaker who was a merchant in Norwich. Her maiden name was Gurney. In 1800 she married Joseph Fry, a London banker. During their life together, she had eleven children.

Her large family took up much of her time. But her deep religious beliefs made her help others. It was that force which had taken her to Newgate Prison when she heard of the conditions of the prisoners.

In 1817 she again went to the prison. She set up a school there for the children. The women were taught to sew and make simple garments. Often Mrs Fry read to them from the Bible. Her strong faith was felt by all of those who met her. She sat quietly with women who were waiting to be transported. An even more heart-rending task was to sit in the condemned cell with those who were awaiting execution.

As a woman of determination and ability, she brought the bad conditions to light. Groups of rich and important people were taken to the prison. There they were shown the state of affairs which existed. Some helped her to make a campaign for improvement. Others believed that prisoners deserved the harsh treatment which they received.

It was some time before her work brought many results. However, one person who took notice was Sir Robert Peel. He was sure that law, prisons and the attitude to crime and criminals needed a change. In the 1820s he was Home Secretary, the minister of the government who is particularly responsible for the keeping of law and order. Through his work, reforms were made. Prisons were inspected and standards were raised. The number of capital offences was reduced.

In 1829 the Metropolitan Police Force was introduced. These men, known as 'Peelers' or 'Bobbies' were to reduce crime by patrolling the streets. Gradually they were successful and became accepted as a vital part of London's life, preventing lawbreaking and helping thousands.

Mrs Fry travelled in many European countries, inspecting prisons and their conditions. She became famous for her work. By the time of her death in 1845, large improvements had been made in Britain.

1815
Waterloo

THE LAST ACT

Napoleon's final defeat: Splendid victory for the Allies: A close fought battle

The squadrons of French cavalry prepared for another charge. Orders were shouted and horses bucked and turned as they were drawn into line. The riders looked magnificent in their uniforms. Then they broke again into a canter. Shouts and cheers were raised. Sabres were waved and lances lowered. They came nearer and nearer to the British line.

This was the fourth attack that the British infantry had taken. They were formed up into a square, waiting. Their muskets were rested until the French approached. The soldiers knew that they must hold their position. The square must not be broken. If they did not keep their ground they would be slaughtered by the cavalry. Inside the square lay the dead and the wounded. They had been dragged there after the last attack.

The Frenchmen swept in. They were met by a hail of fire. Horses reared up and some rolled over. Cavalrymen were thrown through the air. A few made gaps in the line of the square, but these were quickly filled. One horseman actually galloped right into the middle of the square before he was brought down and bayoneted. The noise, confusion and smoke were terrible. Then the cavalry withdrew. Another attack had failed.

The date was 18th June 1815 and one of the greatest land battles was taking place. There was desperate fighting in Belgium, near a small village whose name has since become famous – Waterloo.

France had been raised to a great position of success and military power by the Emperor Napoleon. His armies had conquered many lands and his name became feared and respected. Yet by 1814 his enemies had closed in on France and he was overthrown. He abdicated on 11th April. The Allies who had defeated him were faced with a problem. What should they do with him?

Napoleon was allowed to keep the title of 'Emperor'. He was permitted to go to the small island of Elba in the Mediterranean and become its ruler. Thus they hoped that he would cause no further trouble in Europe.

Wellington passes some of his troops

The centre of the British Army

But a man of Napoleon's ability and ambition could not be satisfied with such a position. He wished to lead his country once again. His plans had not been fully achieved. Therefore in February 1815 he escaped from Elba. He landed near Cannes in southern France. At first there were few supporters. But gradually more and more men flocked to his colours.

From 20th March 1815 Napoleon was once again Emperor in the French capital. He realised that he had surprised his enemies. To gain the greatest effect he needed to strike at them quickly. Soon the Emperor had about 130,000 fighting men ready for war.

Opposed to him in Europe were the armies of various countries which had fought in the recent war. But in 1815 only two armies were prepared for fighting. One was a Prussian force under the command of Marshal Blücher, comprising more than 140,000 men. The other was an army of Hanoverian, Dutch, Belgian and British troops under the leadership of the Duke of Wellington. The Russian and Austrian armies were engaged in different parts of Europe and could lend no help.

Napoleon struck eastwards against his enemies. He wished to separate and defeat the two armies and then to capture Brussels. The first attacks were made on the Prussians at Ligny and on Wellington's army at Quatre Bras. The British force held and the Prussians fell back towards them. On 18th June, Wellington held a position near the village of Waterloo, while the Prussians re-formed some kilometres away. Blücher sent a message to the British commander that he would arrive as soon as possible.

Napoleon's army around Waterloo amounted to some 71,000 men, with 246 cannon. He dispatched one of his commanders, Grouchy, with 32,000 men and 108 guns to deal with the Prussians. Then he prepared to attack Wellington's position. The Duke had 68,000 men under his command, of whom 25,000 were British. They were supported by 156 guns.

Many of the French were experienced soldiers who had fought in several campaigns. With some of Napoleon's famous marshals they had rejoined their Emperor when he had returned from Elba. However, others were young and untried, because of the cost of Napoleon's many campaigns. A number of the British soldiers were young and inexperienced and had not been in action before, but some were veterans of the Peninsula Campaign.

Wellington had planned his defence well. On the right was a large house, called Hougomont and on the left a farmhouse called La Haye Sainte. The French began their attack during

Napoleon and the Old Guard

the morning. They advanced in columns on the British lines with the idea of defeating them before the Prussians arrived to help. Again and again they poured forward in attack, with the support of heavy artillery fire.

British artillery bombarded the French as they advanced. Wellington's infantry were drawn up in squares and showed wonderful steadiness. In the square, the infantry faced outwards along the four sides, making an unbroken wall of fire. Then, as the French fell back after each attack, the Duke ordered his cavalry to launch charges at them.

The fighting at Hougomont and La Haye Sainte was particularly fierce. The farm was lost, then retaken in close hand-to-hand conflict. Hougomont was shelled to ruins but the Guards defending it did not give way. Elsewhere, strong cavalry charges led to heavy casualties on both sides.

By the early evening Napoleon's attacks had not succeeded. He realised that little time was left. Then the first of the Prussian troops were seen approaching. The Emperor called up his Imperial Guard to make one supreme effort. Under the command of Marshal Ney they advanced, 6,000 strong, in an attempt to capture the hill of Mont St. Jean which lay in the centre of Wellington's position.

When they were close to the British line a volley of musket fire was poured at them. They had never been defeated before, but now they stopped. Then, as the British charged at them, they turned and broke. The battle was almost over. More Prussians arrived after fighting their way forward all day against Grouchy's men. Blücher had kept his promise to support Wellington. The two men met near a farm-house and shook hands.

Napoleon had retreated towards Paris. He then abdicated for a second time and surrendered to the captain of a British ship at the port of Rochefort. This time he was sent far away. The Emperor was exiled to the small island of St. Helena, in the South Atlantic Ocean. He lived there until his death in 1821.

In Britain, the news of victory at Waterloo was greeted by cheering crowds. It had been won at a heavy cost, for the British alone suffered almost 7,000 casualties. However, the survivors could say with pride that they had been there. A grateful government allowed that day's service to count as the equivalent of two years towards their pensions. On the muster-rolls of their regiments they were known, in future, as 'Waterloo-men'.

Wellington, the great national hero, later came back to enter politics, becoming Prime Minister in 1828. He died in 1852 but the nation never forgot The Iron Duke.

1819
Peterloo

YEOMANRY CHASE CROWD

Demonstration ends in violence: Many casualties: Who started it?

The year 1819 was a time of political upset in Britain. It lay in the period which followed the Napoleonic Wars. Many people in the land were suffering from hardships. Wages were low and prices were high. There was considerable unemployment. Some men believed strongly that there should be political reform. Then the voices of the sufferers would be heard and laws could be passed to improve their conditions.

For many years in Britain it has been the custom to protest against bad conditions by holding political meetings. Usually these are orderly. Speeches are made. Resolutions are passed. Then, people's complaints are heard and often matters are put right.

However, some public meetings end in violence. One that did has become famous in British history. It happened on 16th August 1819 and is known as 'Peterloo'. The name is given because the memory of another violent battle, Waterloo, was still in people's minds. And the event occurred in St. Peter's Fields, Manchester.

The misery felt by many people at that time was shown by large attendances at public meetings. A familiar figure at many of these was Henry Hunt. Born in 1773 he was a Radical in politics. That meant that he wanted great changes and reforms to be made in society.

The crowd as the cavalry rode in

He was nicknamed 'Orator' Hunt because he was a fine speaker when addressing crowds of his supporters. On two occasions he had stood for Parliament, though without success. He was to play a vital part in the events at Peterloo.

Meetings were held in a number of places. One took place in Manchester during January. In June, they were held at Leeds, Glasgow, Stockport and Blackburn. The speeches made were strong in their tone. They were attacks on the government and its policies. Some speakers reminded the audiences of how the French had overthrown their government in the Revolution of 1789.

Ministers of the government were worried. They feared that there could be an outbreak of violence. Mobs might run riot, killing people and doing great damage. Therefore magistrates were asked to keep a careful watch on any meetings which were held in their area.

But the reformers were determined to make their opinions heard. They believed that the government was trying to stop free speech. Those living in Manchester invited Henry Hunt to address a great meeting there. They chose a large, open space known as St. Peter's Fields. Before the meeting, groups of reformers met. They practised marching together in order. Magistrates thought that this would help them to become a fighting force. But the leaders claimed that the drill was merely intended to help them keep together with discipline.

The date of the meeting was arranged for 16th August. The local magistrates feared what might happen. Therefore they sent men to St. Peter's Fields beforehand. Their task was to clear the area of all stones and objects which could be used for violence.

On the day, thousands of people came in from miles around. They marched in from the surrounding villages. Some were accompanied by bands. Many carried banners, with such mottoes as 'No Corn Laws' and 'Vote by Ballot'. One said 'Hunt and Liberty'. All made their way to the meeting place. The scene was like a grand holiday. In the middle of St. Peter's Fields, two wagons had been placed.

A struggle in the crowd

A platform was erected on them. As the groups of marchers arrived to cheers and singing, they moved in and took up their positions near the platform. About one o'clock, 'Orator' Hunt came to the scene. He travelled in a coach. By that time the crowd was so thick that it was not easy to reach the wagons. However, he did so while bands played the National Anthem and *Rule Britannia*. Then, three cheers were given for him as the meeting began.

The chairman of the local magistrates was William Hulton. He and his other officers had taken up a position in a nearby house. Many of them expected that trouble might come during the meeting. But they were not sure what it might be. They had taken many precautions. Some 200 special constables were there. Some companies of infantry were close by. Also there were several groups of cavalry at the ready. Some were of the Cheshire and Manchester Yeomanry. Others were of the 15th Hussars. The soldiers were under the command of Colonel L'Estrange.

By the time that Henry Hunt began to address the meeting, the magistrates were

Manchester Heroes: *a contemporary cartoon depicting the scene in St. Peter's Fields*

very worried. It appeared that more than 50,000 people had gathered in St. Peter's Fields. Several local citizens feared that violence might break out at any moment. In reality, the crowd were in good order. At last, William Hulton decided that the leaders should be arrested. Therefore a warrant was signed and handed to Joseph Nadin, the Deputy-Chief Constable. Nadin looked at the packed mass in front of him. He said that he could not arrest the leaders unless soldiers helped him. Therefore, some cavalry of the Yeomanry were ordered forward. At that point the terrible events began. It is difficult to know the true details. Some said that the Yeomanry cut at people with their swords as they moved towards the carts. Others stated that the crowd first threw stones and hit out with sticks.

There was great violence. The Hussars were ordered to ride in and help the Yeomanry. People in the crowd ran and shouted, were trampled and struck. When the soldiers reached the platform, they arrested Hunt and several others. Then they seized many of the flags and banners which had been brought by the reformers. Within about ten minutes, it was all over. Dead and injured people lay in many places. Eleven had been killed and some four hundred badly hurt.

There was a great public outcry when the news became known. Rightly or wrongly, most blame was put upon the magistrates and the cavalry. The ministers of the government feared the strong movement towards Reform. Therefore they quickly passed measures to limit public meetings, known as the Six Acts.

In 1820, Henry Hunt and several other reformers were brought to trial. They were charged with high treason over the events that led to Peterloo. The 'Orator' was found guilty and sent to prison for two and a half years. But that August day in Manchester is still discussed. It was a famous event in the struggle for Reform.

1830
The Liverpool and Manchester Railway

GEORGE STEPHENSON TRIUMPHS

Triumph and tragedy: Man's fastest means of travel: Death of Mr Huskisson

It was like a great festival day. Thousands of local men, women and children had come along to watch. The event had been well advertised. Flags and banners waved above the excited crowds. There were very few occasions in their lives when they could see such a bright spectacle. And there were some famous people present. The Prime Minister himself, the great Duke of Wellington was there.

The date was 15th September 1830. The important occasion was taking place in the north of England. It was the opening day of a railway which had been built between Liverpool and Manchester. Large preparations were made at both places because the line was of great importance to their trade. Eight locomotives were made ready to take part in the opening ceremonies. They were to travel from Liverpool to Manchester. At their destination, a banquet was prepared for all of the important visitors.

From the early hours of the morning, spectators began to line the route. They found the best positions on hillsides and bridges from which they could watch. The trains were divided into two groups. One took the up-line and the other used the down-line. Then the great journey began. The crowds cheered and buzzed with excitement as they recognised some of the important persons who were present.

At intervals along the route supplies of water and coal were available for the engines. One of these was at a point called Park-side.

The train carrying the Duke of Wellington stopped there to take on more fuel. Most of the passengers got down from their small carriages for a short break. As they recognised their friends who had been travelling in different parts of the train, they walked over to talk to them. It was an easy and relaxing time for everyone.

One of the passengers was a Member of Parliament for Liverpool. His name was William Huskisson and his wife had accompanied him on the ride towards Manchester.

The Father of English Railways, George Stephenson

He had previously been Colonial Secretary in the Duke of Wellington's government but had resigned in 1828 after a disagreement with the leader. Another Member of Parliament decided to bring the two men together again. Therefore he took Mr Huskisson towards Wellington. They shook hands and began talking.

At that moment a tragedy occurred. Suddenly, another train, drawn by the *Rocket* appeared on the other line. There was a general shout of warning. Groups of people quickly leapt out of the way as the locomotive bore down on them. Its appearance had come as a complete surprise. In the confusion, Huskisson tripped and fell. The engine passed over his left leg and thigh, giving him terrible injuries.

The accident came as a great shock to all of those who saw it. The event spoiled one of the greatest days in the story of Britain's transport. Poor Mr Huskisson was carried by train to a nearby village. But before long, he died. This terrible happening was carefully noted by those people who were opponents of railways.

When the procession reached Manchester, a number of visitors alighted. They were given food. But because of the accident everyone was quiet. Some passengers stayed in their carriages until it was time to return. Then the trains made their way back to Liverpool and arrived there in the evening.

The accident caused a great deal of unhappiness. Yet overall, the day was a splendid success. It showed the cleverness and ability of one particular man. He was a famous engineer. Often he is known as 'The Father of English Railways'. His name was George Stephenson.

During the early years of the nineteenth century important changes occurred in transport. The steam engine, which had been de-

The 'Rocket' at the Rainhill Trials, 1829

The railway crossing Chat Moss

veloped throughout the eighteenth century, was applied to railways. Small locomotives were built, powered by steam. It was soon shown that they could run easily on rails and could pull heavy loads.

There were several pioneers of this work. One brilliant engineer was Richard Trevithick. Another was William Hedley. But the greatest of them all was George Stephenson. He was born in 1781, the son of a colliery labourer. When he grew up, Stephenson worked at a colliery. His interest lay in steam engines.

When a line from Stockton to Darlington was planned in the 1820s, Stephenson was appointed to be its engineer. The railway was opened in 1825 and was a great success. In the following year, a line was planned from Liverpool to Manchester. The two cities were great trading centres. The changes of the Industrial Revolution led to a need for better transport. As more and more goods were produced, they had to be carried swiftly and safely. Roads were poor and canals were slow. Therefore the idea of a railway appealed to some businessmen.

Stephenson was offered the job of chief engineer. He then showed his remarkable ability by planning the line. It had to pass across some very difficult country. Viaducts,

cuttings, bridges and tunnels were constructed. A peat marsh had to be crossed. In carrying out the work, Stephenson proved himself to be a great civil engineer.

Then came the choice of engine for the railway. The directors of the line held a competition to see which locomotive was the best. The tests were held at Rainhill, near Manchester, in 1829. Of the four engines which took part, one was the *Rocket*. This engine was Stephenson's own and had been built by his son, Robert. It won the test, which is usually known as the Rainhill Trials. At one stage, the locomotive reached 48 k.p.h.

Thus all was set for the opening day of the great new railway. The important visitors were invited to attend. Posters and advertisements were read by thousands of ordinary people. They, too, decided to come to the great occasion. Some merely came to watch. Some came to hiss and boo the politicians who were being slow in bringing in reforms. Others were opposed to the new, noisy and dirty trains. They wished to show disapproval.

The death of Mr Huskisson was soon forgotten. Over the next twenty years railways were built in many parts of Britain. Stephenson was a pioneer of work which brought changes to an industrial land.

1832
The Great Reform Bill

RADICAL CHANGE IN VOTING

A victory for the Reformers: Thousands get the vote: Scenes of excitement in Parliament

There was uproar in Parliament. Many older members could hardly remember any previous scene which matched it. Men shouted and cheered. They clapped their hands and stamped their feet. The Bill had been passed. After years of struggle, there was victory for those who wanted change. They believed that a new age would begin.

But several members stood at one side and shook their heads. From their faces it was obvious that they were unhappy. They believed that the Bill should have been thrown out. The country would suffer. A system which had lasted for many years had been thrown away. They felt that there were too many men in Parliament with new ideas. The old ways had been good enough. Why change them? However, change had come, The year was 1832 and a famous Act of Parliament had just been passed. It is usually known as the First, or Great Reform Bill. The passing of the measure is one of the great landmarks in British history.

A cartoonist's view of old elections

For many years, Parliament had not truly represented the people of Britain. Compared with the present day, few men were entitled to vote. Members were chosen by methods which were often unfair. Many large areas had no representatives at all. The organisation of Parliament had changed little since the Middle Ages. Those who held power there were mainly the great landowners and the aristocracy. Thus a few men were able to govern the lives of millions of their countrymen. The system had lasted through the eighteenth century. However, by the early nineteenth century it was obviously unfair.

A particular reason for this was the coming of the Industrial Revolution. By 1830 there had been vast changes in Britain. Cities with factories had sprung up in parts of the Midlands and the North. More and more people made their living from industry and trade. Britain was no longer a mainly farming area. The population had grown enormously.

The old system of choosing the country's Parliament was therefore out of date. The large, growing areas of industry were not properly represented. Yet, some ancient places, which now had hardly any inhabitants, continued to return members.

Two classes of people were very interested in gaining the vote. One was the middle class. Men here were often those who had made money from the expanding industries, like iron, coal and cotton. Some had gained wealth from overseas trade. But many had no vote. The other group consisted of some men of the working class. They were usually skilled craftsmen, men of good intelligence. The nation made good profits from their work. They had an interest in the affairs of their country, yet no say in its government.

At the end of the eighteenth century the idea of reforming Parliament had been discussed. But the coming of the French Revolution in 1789 had put a stop to any change. The land-owning interests feared that a similar uprising might occur in Britain. Therefore they were strongly opposed to giving the vote to new areas and new groups of the population.

After the wars with France came to an end in 1815, there was a strong movement for

An election scene in the late eighteenth century

Reform. Many people considered that the passing of the Corn Laws in that year was an example of how the landowners looked after their own interests through passing laws in Parliament. They were angered by such unfairness.

However, for a number of years many politicians resisted change. The Tory Party had a majority in the House of Commons and in the House of Lords. Therefore they were able to stop all plans to alter the system. Nevertheless, some Tories and many Whigs gradually came to favour change. Therefore, by the late 1820s, Reform of Parliament became a main point of debate.

At the end of 1830, the Tory government, with the Duke of Wellington as Prime Minister, was voted out of office. Its place was taken by a Whig government, under the leadership of Lord Grey. In March 1831, the Whigs introduced a Reform Bill. The Bill aroused enormous interest in Britain. Men everywhere discussed it. Merchants and labourers, engineers and squires had long debates about the measure. Some were pleased and some were angry. Public meetings were held. Processions marched through the streets and pamphlets were widely read.

The suggestions put forward in the bill were concerned with two main reforms. The first one was a change in constituencies, that is, the areas represented by members. Altogether, there were 658 of them. Some of the old boroughs were to be abolished. Other

The House of Commons in 1832

boroughs, which had had two members, should have only one. Because of this, there would be 143 seats to give to other constituencies. It was proposed to give them mainly to the large industrial areas, especially in the Midlands and the North.

The second main reform was concerned with who should be allowed to vote. The right was now to be given to those men in boroughs and towns who owned or rented some property. The property had to be worth at least £10 a year in rent. In the counties, a man would generally need to own land worth at least £10 a year to gain the vote. Thus, thousands more men were offered the vote, but they were not those of the working class. The Reform Bill helped those of the middle class.

At first, the House of Lords refused to pass the Bill when the Commons sent it to them. There were many Tories among the Lords. They felt that change would bring more harm than good. Some of them believed that there could be no better system than the one which existed. The mood of many reformers grew stern. They were bitterly angry that the Lords had taken this attitude. Therefore meetings and demonstrations were held in many parts of Britain. Sometimes they led to violence. A number of people were prepared for revolution if Reform did not come. The Duke of Wellington, who was opposed to Reform, had his windows broken in London. At Nottingham, the castle was burned. In Bristol, a mob controlled the city for a time.

At length, in June 1832, the Lords allowed the Bill to pass. There was celebration in many places. But over the next few years, people came to realise that it was only a beginning. Much remained to be done. Many thousands of men, and all women, still had no vote. Only one man out of every six in Britain was entitled to choose Members of Parliament.

The period of government by the Whigs between 1830 and 1841 saw the passing of many social reforms. They were very much needed at that time but probably the most important of them all was the Great Reform Bill of 1832.

1833
The Abolition of Slavery

BRITAIN SHOWS THE WAY

An end to slavery in the Empire: Freedom for West Indian Negroes: Another Government reform

The Negroes listened carefully to the white man who sat in front of them. He was explaining an important matter. Point by point, he was explaining the way in which it would affect their lives. Some asked questions. They nodded gravely at the answers.

The year was 1833 and the scene was taking place many hundreds of kilometres away from Britain. It was on the island of Jamaica. Yet an act passed by the British Parliament had just made a vital difference to the lives of the men in the group.

One of them was the rich owner of a sugar-plantation. He was the white man. All of the Negroes were poor. In fact they were owned by the planter. They were his slaves. He had bought some of them. Several others had been bought by his father, years before, when he owned the plantation. Now he was telling them that they were no longer to be his slaves. Most would be free men within a year. The Parliament in London had passed a Bill which would bring an end to slavery within the British Empire.

A slave trade to Jamaica had existed for many years. Europeans opened up the way to the New World from the end of the fifteenth century. They explored and settled in Central and South America. They landed in North America and established themselves there. Colonies were set up on various islands of the West Indies.

Before long, there was a need for a force of men and women to labour in the new settlements. Sugar and cotton became two important products of the New World. Those were days before machinery was in use. Often the climate was very hot and Europeans were not able to carry out the long and hard work needed on the plantations.

The people found to be best suited to the work were Negroes from Africa. They were carried to the American continent by what was known as the Triangular Trade. Ships sailed on the first side of the triangle from Europe to West Africa. In Britain, the ports of Liverpool and Bristol were well known starting places. Cargoes of goods, such as pots and pans, spirits and ornaments were carried. They were exchanged for Negroes who had often been captured in tribal wars. Many were bought from Arab slave traders.

On the second side of the triangle, the slaves were transported across the Atlantic Ocean. This was the 'Middle Passage'. The slaves were kept in dreadful conditions, often chained below decks. Many died on the voyage. When they arrived in the New World, they were sold, usually by auction. The ship's captain then often bought a cargo of sugar, tobacco, cotton or rum which he carried back to Europe. This was the third side of the triangle. The round trip showed a handsome profit.

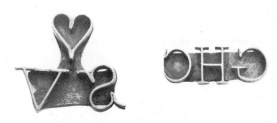

Slave brands

Going on board a slave ship

However, in Britain during the later eighteenth century, there was a strong movement to stop the trade in slaves. It was led by several men of strong religious beliefs. In their view, trading in human beings was totally wrong. No Christian should take part in such a business.

One of the best known opponents of slavery was William Wilberforce. Born in 1759, he was a Member of Parliament for Yorkshire between 1784 and 1812. He spoke out boldly against the trade. Wilberforce was widely respected. Therefore many people listened carefully to his views. The campaign which he and his friends launched had gradual success. They organised meetings of protest. Pamphlets were printed and issued. Appeals were made to Parliament.

In 1807, a step forward was taken. The government forbade British subjects to take part in the slave trade. Also, no ships which carried the British flag were allowed to carry slaves. But it was a long job to persuade other countries to stop their ships from trading in human cargoes.

By 1830, France, Portugal and Spain agreed to stop. The latter two countries were given large grants of British money for doing so. However, the government of the United States would not agree. Many of the slaves were used on the plantations of the southern states. A large number were carried in American ships. Therefore, they would not forbid the trade to their own people.

Wilberforce would not give up the struggle. The anti-slavery group wished to abolish the trade altogether. Therefore they continued their campaign. One of them was Thomas Fowell Buxton, who had married a sister of Elizabeth Fry. In 1823 he asked the House of

Commons to take a step forward by freeing all children born to slaves. But this was not done at once.

However, the government brought in measures to improve the treatment of slaves. They met with great opposition. Some MP's favoured the slave system. These men spoke up on behalf of the planters in the West Indies. It was suggested that they would lose money and trade if their slaves were set free. Also it

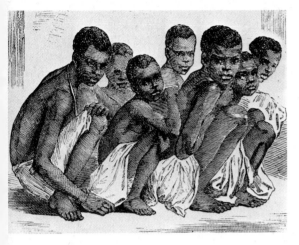

Slaves packed below in a 'slaver'

was stated that the planters themselves knew more about what was good for negroes than the English Parliament did.

At length, the government decided to intervene. In 1833 they brought in a plan. They hoped to please both the planters and the anti-slavery movement. All slaves within the British Empire were to be freed, over a period of twelve months. Money would be given to their owners, as compensation. At first, the government offered the sum of £15 million. During the long debate, some members persuaded them to raise the figure to £20 million. This was to be a free payment. The government had said that the average selling price of a slave was £38 and they were offering £37 10s. William Wilberforce was not present at the moment of victory. He had retired in 1825, suffering from ill-health. His death came in 1833, just a short time before the Bill was passed.

Thus Britain made an important move towards reform. She was the first country which tried to stamp out slavery. The steps taken were gradually successful. Although slaves had their personal freedom, they remained with their employers as apprentices for a time. However, the slave trade was continued, though on a smaller scale. It was illegal, but a ship's captain could still make a fortune if he was prepared to take risks. Over the following years, British warships patrolled the seas and tried to stop slavers whenever they found them.

One country which still objected strongly to having its ships stopped and searched was the U.S.A. Slavery continued there until the 1860's, when it became a big issue in the American Civil War. Then, at the end of the war in 1865, all that nation's slaves were freed at once.

1834
The Tolpuddle Martyrs

SAVAGE SENTENCE FOR DORSET MEN

Farm labourers to be transported for forming an illegal union: A harsh punishment?

Tolpuddle is a small village which lies deep in the Dorset countryside. It is situated about 11 kilometres from the county town of Dorchester. In 1834, an event occurred there which concerned a number of farm labourers. At first, it was local news and the centre of conversation. Gradually the news spread until people all over Great Britain became interested in what was going on in that area of Dorset. Within a short time, Tolpuddle became a place to be remembered.

That period was a time of great hardship in some parts of the English countryside. Farm workers have always been among the lowest paid of employees. By 1834, the wages paid to agricultural workers were very low indeed. Often they amounted only to about nine shillings (45p) each week. In Dorset, wages were less than in some other counties. And at the village of Tolpuddle they were among the worst in the county.

The 1830s were years of reform. This means that steps were taken to improve many of the conditions under which people lived. In Britain, a number of reformers wished to see better standards of living for ordinary men and women. In Tolpuddle, many of the farm labourers believed that they should be able to improve and reform their working conditions. Some of them, during 1833 approached the local vicar. They told him about their hardships. He helped them to come to an agreement with their employers, the local farmers. The agreement was that they should be paid not less than nine or ten shillings (45 or 50p) each week.

However, the harvest that year was a poor one. Therefore the farmers felt that they could not offer so much. They suggested the figure of seven shillings (35p) per week. There was talk that it might even be reduced to six shillings (30p) later. This news brought both disappointment and fear to the village labourers. They believed that their employers had cheated them. Also they feared that their families would soon face starvation. Some of the workers wanted to unite to meet their troubles.

In those days there were no trade unions, in the modern sense. However, Robert Owen was trying to persuade working men to form into organised groups. Owen was a rich and influential man. He believed that if workers formed unions, they would be able to control employers. In 1834 he formed the giant 'Grand National Consolidated Trades Union'. He hoped that it would control the country's industry and trade.

In Tolpuddle, one of the labourers was named George Loveless. He was an honest, hard-working and religious man. He had heard of Owen's ideas and tried to form a union. Loveless obtained a book of union rules. Then he persuaded others to join.

There was a small, secret ceremony held at which new members were introduced. They were blindfolded for part of the time. One of the articles used in the ceremony was a skeleton. It was meant to show how serious the whole business was. The entry fee was one shilling (5p). Members also had to pay one penny ($\frac{1}{2}$p) a week. The local magistrates heard about what was going on and were very worried. A notice was posted by them in Tolpuddle. It warned men against forming illegal unions.

CAUTION.

WHEREAS it has been represented to us from several quarters, that mischievous and designing Persons have been for some time past, endeavouring to induce, and have induced, many Labourers in various Parishes in this County, to attend Meetings, and to enter into Illegal Societies or Unions, to which they bind themselves by unlawful oaths, administered secretly by Persons concealed, who artfully deceive the ignorant and unwary,—WE, the undersigned Justices think it our duty to give this PUBLIC NOTICE and CAUTION, that all Persons may know the danger they incur by entering into such Societies.

ANY PERSON who shall become a Member of such a Society, or take any Oath, or assent to any Test or Declaration not authorized by Law—

Any Person who shall administer, or be present at, or consenting to the administering or taking any Unlawful Oath, or who shall cause such Oath to be administered, although not actually present at the time—

Any Person who shall not reveal or discover any Illegal Oath which may have been administered, or any Illegal Act done or to be done—

Any Person who shall induce, or endeavour to persuade any other Person to become a Member of such Societies,

WILL BECOME

Guilty of Felony,

AND BE LIABLE TO BE

Transported for Seven Years.

ANY PERSON who shall be compelled to take such an Oath, unless he shall declare the same within four days, together with the whole of what he shall know touching the same, will be liable to the same Penalty.

Any Person who shall directly or indirectly maintain correspondence or intercourse with such Society, will be deemed Guilty of an Unlawful Combination and Confederacy, and on Conviction before one Justice, on the Oath of one Witness, be liable to a Penalty of TWENTY POUNDS, or to be committed to the Common Gaol or House of Correction, for THREE CALENDAR MONTHS; or if proceeded against by Indictment, may be CONVICTED OF FELONY, and be TRANSPORTED FOR SEVEN YEARS.

Any Person who shall knowingly permit any Meeting of any such Society to be held in any House, Building, or other Place, shall for the first offence be liable to the Penalty of FIVE POUNDS; and for every other offence committed after Conviction, be deemed Guilty of such Unlawful Combination and Confederacy, and on Conviction before one Justice, on the Oath of one Witness, be liable to a Penalty of TWENTY POUNDS, or to Commitment to the Common Gaol or House of Correction, FOR THREE CALENDAR MONTHS; or if proceeded against by Indictment may be

CONVICTED OF FELONY,
And Transported for SEVEN YEARS.

COUNTY OF DORSET,	C. B. WOLLASTON,	HENRY FRAMPTON,
Dorchester Division.	JAMES FRAMPTON,	RICHD. TUCKER STEWARD,
	WILLIAM ENGLAND,	WILLIAM R. CHURCHILL,
February 22d. 1834.	THOS. DADE,	AUGUSTUS FOSTER.
	JNO. MORTON COLSON,	

G. CLARK, PRINTER, CORNHILL, DORCHESTER.

A poster warning of the dangers of joining an illegal association or Union

A group of convicts in Tasmania

which at that time, was a crime. However, George Loveless and his friends did not believe that they had done anything wrong.

On 24th February 1834, six of the labourers in Tolpuddle were approached by the local constable. He had a warrant for their arrest. They had all taken the oath. The men were George Loveless and James, his brother; Thomas Standfield and John, his son; James Hammett and James Brine. They were accused under the Unlawful Oaths Act of 1797.

They all walked into Dorchester, the county town of Dorset, to appear before the magistrates. Another labourer who had taken the oath was brought forward and recognised them. Then they were taken into custody and put in prison cells to wait for a trial. The news came as a shock to the people of the village, who did not believe that any crime had been committed.

The trial began on 15th March, in Dorchester. It was obvious from the start that the local authorities were determined to find the men guilty. They believed that the labourers were a threat to society. If they were allowed to go free, their ideas could overthrow the life of those who owned property and were employers. The jury were a group of men who were hardly likely to show sympathy for the accused men.

At the end of the trial, the six labourers were found guilty. The judge sentenced them to transportation for seven years. He was determined to make an example of them. Thus, other men would not form into unions which could upset the way of life of the time. The verdict and the sentence were severe. Meetings of protest were soon held. A large one took place in north London, where some 50,000 people met. They marched to Westminster and presented a petition. The government was worried and called out units of the army, as well as special constables, to keep the peace.

The six labourers were transported. Five were sent on prison ships to Sydney, in Australia. The remaining one, George Loveless, was later sent to Tasmania, which was then called Van Diemen's Land. They all met very hard conditions there and were treated as if they were hardened criminals.

After two years of pressure from their friends at home, the government agreed to release the men. They were granted a free pardon and a passage back to England. In those days communications were very bad and some of the men only heard of their pardons by reading old newspapers. Five returned in 1837, but James Hammett did not come back until the next year. He lived on in Dorset until 1891. The others and their families went first to Essex, then later emigrated to Canada.

The case was an important point in the story of working men seeking the right to join a union. The men involved suffered a great deal and have become known as the 'Tolpuddle Martyrs'. They were part of a campaign for men's rights which was later taken up by the Chartists and, towards the end of the nineteenth century, the dockers in their famous strike of 1889.

1838
The Coronation

GOD SAVE THE QUEEN!

Long May She Reign!: Great crowds see our young Queen: Her wonderful day

On 28th June 1838, thousands of people crowded into a number of London's streets. They lined up on each side of the roads, waiting for a procession to pass by. The day was important for Britain, for it marked the coronation of the young Queen Victoria. Men, women and children jostled in the streets to get a good position.

Many had been waiting for hours.

Soon after 10 am, those standing outside Buckingham Palace were able to see the royal procession as it left on its journey to Westminster Abbey. The sight was very imposing and full of colour. There were mounted trumpeters, squadrons of horse-guards, bands, carriages, yeomen of the guard and many others. Their uniforms were bright on a day that was dry, although it had begun rather dull.

The young Queen being crowned

Victoria with two politicians – (left) Lord Melbourne and (right) Lord Grey

All eyes were turned on the Queen's state-coach. It was drawn by eight cream-coloured horses. Victoria sat inside, with one of her ladies-in-waiting. She was a small figure of a girl, slender and hardly 1 metre 50 centimetres tall. She smiled at the crowds, but looked a little tense. The day would prove to be very hard for someone who was only nineteen years old.

The procession moved on, through cheering crowds. It passed along Constitution Hill, Piccadilly, St. James's Street, Pall Mall, Whitehall and Parliament Street. Soon after 11.30 am the Queen arrived at Westminster Abbey. She moved slowly into the great building and the long ceremony began.

At the west end of the Choir, 400 people were crowded into a gallery which had been erected specially for the occasion. More than 600 were in another at the east end. Both galleries were draped with crimson cloth lined with gold. Under the Abbey's centre tower was a raised platform, resting on a purple and gold carpet. It was covered with a cloth of gold. In the middle stood a large, decorated throne, which faced the altar. All around were seated famous people. There were politicians, noblemen and foreign ambassadors. Their eyes looked carefully at the young girl who was about to be crowned Queen of a great nation.

Victoria was escorted by her mother, the Duchess of Kent, as she came in through the west door. There, she was met by several officials who had tasks to perform during the ceremony. People could see that she wore a crimson velvet robe, with ermine, fur and gold lace. The long train was carried by eight ladies. Her hair was arranged simply and on her head was a small crown. She looked nervous but moved with remarkable dignity.

As the ceremony progressed, a crown was placed on the young Queen's head. It was a special one, less than half the weight of the crown previously used. Diamonds, sapphires, emeralds, rubies and pearls made a glittering display. Then an act of homage was made. Various lords came forward to kneel and kiss Victoria's hand. She moved forward to offer her hand to Lord Rolle, an old man who found difficulty in mounting the steps. Those watching her thus noticed how she spared thought for others.

At length, the coronation came to a close. The time was just after 3 pm. The Queen returned to Buckingham Palace where she later attended a dinner-party for 100 guests. All over the capital there were celebrations. The Duke of Wellington gave a grand ball at Apsley House. A fair was held in Hyde Park, with fireworks in the evening. The day was one of great celebration but was very tiring for the young Victoria.

She had come to the Throne in the previous year upon the death of her uncle, William IV. He was the second son of George III. William and his wife, Adelaide, had no children, therefore the claim passed to the next son and his children. The third son was Edward, Duke of Kent, and Victoria was his only child, born in 1819. Edward died when she was young, therefore it was known for some years that she would succeed her uncle.

The news of William's death was brought to Princess Victoria early on the morning of 20th June 1837. The Archbishop of Canterbury and the Lord Chamberlain arrived and asked to see her. They knelt before her in homage to their new Queen.

At that time there were people in Britain who did not believe that the monarchy would last much longer. The previous kings had often been unpopular. Sometimes they attempted to interfere in politics. On other occasions their private lives led to public scandal. There was some support for those who did not want a monarch. They believed that Victoria would find the burdens too great. However, they were mistaken. The young Queen was a woman of great character. She had a re- markable sense of duty and never failed to carry out her tasks. Victoria realised the importance of the position which she held and was determined never to let it down. In the

1840: her wedding day with Prince Albert

early months of her reign, the Queen received great help and advice from Lord Melbourne. He was a Whig in politics and was the Prime Minister. Melbourne was fifty-eight years of age and acted like a father to her.

The Queen soon became popular. The nation was happy when, in 1840, she was married. Her husband was a distant cousin from Saxe- Coburg in Germany. He was Prince Albert and was three months younger than Victoria. When they had met in 1836 they had been attracted to each other. Later, they decided on marriage. The royal wedding, like the Coronation, was a glittering occasion.

Victoria and her husband earned a new respect for the monarchy. They were the pat- tern of a happy family life. Before Albert's death in 1861, nine children were born to them. The Queen was strongly influenced by Albert. He was a thoughtful, quiet man with a strong sense of duty. Together, their lives set the tone for much that went on in the Victorian Age. They were serious in outlook and deeply religious. The people of Britain generally respected and followed their example.

1842
The Mines Act

HELP FOR THE WORKING POOR

Improved working conditions for women and children: Lord Shaftesbury's success: Parliament persuaded to act

The members of the House of Commons listened carefully to the speaker. They respected him. He had the reputation of being a helper of the poor, the needy, the weak and the helpless. Now they were listening as he made a plea for their help. The man who spoke to them was Lord Ashley. He was a serious person. A smile seldom came to his face. The cares of the world seemed to rest on his shoulders. He was dressed in dark clothes and his appearance added to the gloom of what he was saying. Carefully Ashley was pointing out to the Members of Parliament that many children in Britain needed their assistance.

The date was 7th June 1842. Anthony Ashley Cooper, known as Lord Ashley, was talking to Members of Parliament about a report which had been published a short time before. The document showed the dreadful conditions under which many poor people, especially women and children, worked at that time. What it said had come as a shock to many people in Britain.

In 1840 Lord Ashley had asked for a commission of enquiry to be set up. Its task was to find out the conditions of work in the country's coal mines. The commission finished its work and then published a report, which was issued in May 1842. As a result, a Bill was introduced to Parliament. It aimed to stamp out the evils which were shown by the report.

Ashley introduced the Bill. He pointed out that many children began work in coal mines at a very early age. In Shropshire, some were only six years old. Many in Derbyshire were only five. Near Halifax, in Yorkshire, some aged six were taken out of their beds at 4 am to go to work. The same kind of story was told from most of Britain's mining areas.

Then the speaker went on to deal with the work of women in coal mines. He showed that it varied from area to area. In some places, no women were employed. However, in others they were regularly working underground. For

Lord Shaftesbury, friend of the poor

example, they could be found in the West Riding of Yorkshire, in Lancashire and in Cheshire. As he quoted from the Report, Ashley drew attention to conditions in the mines. Many women and children spent long hours working in wet galleries and shafts. There was poor ventilation. They had to drag or carry heavy weights over great distances.

Then he appealed to the other Members of Parliament. He asked them, as 'Christian men and British gentlemen' to help his efforts to stamp out such bad conditions. And they did. A Bill was passed which laid down that no women, or girls or boys under ten years of age should work underground. It was an important measure in improving the standards of life for poor people.

Anthony Ashley Cooper was born in 1801. He was the son of the 6th Earl of Shaftesbury. As a boy, he spent an unhappy childhood. His parents often gave him little attention and left much of his upbringing to an old family nurse. He was educated at Harrow School, then at Christ Church College, Oxford. In 1826, at the age of twenty-five, Ashley entered Parliament as a member of the Tory Party. He at once became very interested in social reform. The rest of his life was spent in trying to help the poor and needy of that time.

One of the great evils of the Industrial Revolution was the way in which women and children had to work in factories and mines. Their labour lasted for long hours, sometimes from eleven to fourteen in a day. The working conditions were often terrible. They carried out their tasks in surroundings of dirt and danger, where little thought was given to many of the human beings who were producing wealth for Britain.

Throughout the nineteenth century, various groups of people set out to improve the standards of life under which the poor existed. The evidence showed plainly that many women and children worked too hard. However, their employers believed that this had to continue. They argued that Britain's position as a growing industrial nation would suffer otherwise.

Parliament passed acts in 1802 and 1819 in an attempt to improve matters. These measures

Children being lowered down a coal mine

tried to limit the hours worked by certain children. However, no one checked carefully that the terms of the acts were carried out. Therefore many employers ignored them.

In 1833 a Factory Act was passed. By that time, Ashley was working hard to bring in reforms. With his friends he believed that the act was a step forward. However, much remained to be done. For the first time, inspectors were appointed to see that the act was obeyed. Yet children aged from nine to thirteen could still be employed for up to nine hours a day. Over the following years Ashley's work continued. After his successful campaign in 1842 for children employed in coal mines, he did not stop.

A Factory Act passed in 1844 put further limits on the amount of time which women and children were allowed to work. Then, three years later, Ashley achieved great success. He played an important part in persuading Parliament to accept the Ten Hours' Bill. All women and all young persons under eighteen years of age were limited to ten hours of work in a day.

After his father's death, Ashley took the title of Lord Shaftesbury. He continued his efforts for the poor and weak in Britain. His life was a fine example of a man who gave his energy to improve conditions for other people. He helped to improve standards in lunatic

Capital and Labour: as portrayed by Punch in 1847

asylums. He helped to stop the use of 'climbing boys' for sweeping chimneys. He brought education to poor children through the Ragged Schools Union.

By the end of his life in 1885, Shaftesbury was famous throughout Britain. He was known as a true friend of the poor. He had helped to remind the nation that the Industrial Revolution could not be allowed to make progress by using women and children like slaves.

1845
The Electric Telegraph

A NEW NETWORK

Murderer trapped by telegraph message: News spreads at high speed: Countries can be linked in a flash

John Tawell had committed a murder. He had killed a woman named Hart in a cottage at Salthill, near Slough. Now he was making his escape. Tawell went to Slough station and bought a first-class ticket to London. The murderer walked along the platform, chose a compartment and climbed into the train. At almost a quarter to eight in the evening the train steamed its way out of the station and headed for London. Tawell relaxed. When he arrived in the great city it would be easy to mingle with the crowds. Soon he would be lost to any pursuers. After the train had arrived at Paddington Station, the criminal got into a passing horse-bus and travelled to the Bank. Tawell then proceeded to the Jerusalem coffee-house. After some time there, he crossed over London Bridge to the Leopard coffee-house. He was giving himself a good alibi by being seen in these places.

Then the murderer went to a lodging-house near Cannon Street. He entered and took a room. But suddenly the door opened. The man who stood there spoke and his words sent a chill through Tawell. He said, 'Haven't you just come from Slough?' The confused answer was, 'No.' At that, the visitor stepped forward and announced that he was a detective. He asked the criminal to come with him.

John Tawell did not know that he had been followed, traced and trapped by a wonderful invention of the nineteenth century. It was the electric telegraph which could flash messages at immense speed. Even as he sat in the train, bound for London, his doom was sealed. A message was sent along the wires which ran beside the line. He had been traced to Slough station. From there, the operator sent these words to Paddington Station: 'A murder has just been committed at Salthill, and the suspected murderer was seen to take a first-class ticket for London by the train which left Slough at 7.42 pm. He is in the garb of a Quaker, with a brown great-coat on, which reaches nearly down to his feet. He is in the last compartment of the second first-class carriage.'

Therefore, when the killer arrived at Paddington, a detective was waiting to follow him. At the lodging-house, he pounced. The murderer was brought to trial, sentenced to death and hanged. People marvelled at the new telegraph which had trapped him. One of them looked at the telegraph wires and said, 'Them's the cords that hung John Tawell.'

Some of the greatest advances seen during the nineteenth century were made in methods of communication. For centuries before, news moved slowly. Sometimes messages were carried by men who travelled on horse-back across country. At coastlines the news was taken on ship to the next land. Thus, communication was very slow and sometimes news took weeks or even months to reach Britain.

At the end of the eighteenth century, a Frenchman named Claud Chappe devised a quicker method of sending messages. He set up a system of message stations across France. Each one had large semaphore arms on the roof. They could be worked to send messages which could be seen by men, using telescopes, in the next station. Thus messages could be sent rapidly across country.

In England, a similar system was set up. It

Professor Charles Wheatstone

The railway telegraph in action

enabled messages to be sent from London to Deal. Later they linked London with Portsmouth and Plymouth. However, a great weakness of the semaphore telegraph was that it could be used only during clear weather. Therefore during the early nineteenth century a number of Europeans made experiments with electric telegraphs. In these, an electric signal was sent along a wire. Thus messages could be relayed.

Two Englishmen became very interested in this form of communication. They were W. F. Cooke and Professor C. Wheatstone. In 1838 they demonstrated an electric telegraph to the directors of the Great Western Railway. Electric signals caused needles on the receiving instrument to move. The needles were made to point at various letters of the alphabet and thus to spell out messages.

The telegraph developed quickly, as new railways were built at that time. Messages and information were essential for the safe running of trains. In 1838, the equipment was installed between West Drayton and Paddington. It was extended as far as Slough in 1842. By the early 1850s there were about 6,400 kilometres of telegraph in Great Britain.

An American named Samuel Morse invented a type of telegraph which relied on sending a series of short or long electrical signals – dots and dashes. Underwater telegraph cables were laid between countries which were separated by water. The first successful one from Britain to France was begun in 1851. Fifteen years later a cable was laid across the Atlantic Ocean. Telegraph offices were opened in the great cities of the World. Thus people were able to learn of important events within hours of their happening. The electric telegraph became one of the most important advances made during the nineteenth century.

1846
The Repeal of the Corn Laws

PEEL SPLITS THE PARTY

Victory for the Free Traders: Corn Laws repealed: Split in Tory ranks

A group of politicians sat talking in a room. Worried looks showed on their faces. They were Tories and were busily discussing their leader. His name was Sir Robert Peel and he was the Prime Minister. It appeared to some of them that his policies had become foolish. They would result in the breaking up of their party. Less than half of the men present were prepared to support the leader. The others felt that they could not do so.

The question under discussion was whether or not the Corn Laws should be abolished. The matter became one of great importance in Victorian Britain. In fact, the year 1846 became one of the turning points of the nineteenth century.

The story of the Corn Laws had begun many years before. It had started at the end of the Napoleonic Wars in 1815. During those wars, British farmers had grown more corn than ever before. They had made great efforts to feed the nation. Thousands of extra acres had been ploughed up and sown with grain crops. However, in 1815 farmers and land-owners were worried. They feared that foreign corn would soon be allowed to come into Britain. Its price would be very cheap. Therefore they would obtain little money for their crops.

The landowners at that time were strongly represented in Parliament. Therefore they ensured that laws were passed to protect their own interests. In 1815 a Corn Law was introduced. It did not allow foreign corn to be brought into Britain until home grown corn had reached a high price. The amount chosen was £4 per quarter, which is about 500 lbs or 227 kilos in weight. Thus, British farmers were sure to get a good price. Foreign corn could not be imported unless there was a serious shortage of home grown supplies.

This policy resulted in a high price for bread. For many years the loaf of bread was expensive for poor people in Britain. At that time, bread was a more important food for the working classes than it is today. Therefore, workmen and their families suffered. Wages were not high, especially in country districts. The Corn Laws led to hardship. Those who owned land and grew crops received a good price. The law protected them by keeping out

Richard Cobden and John Bright,
famous free traders

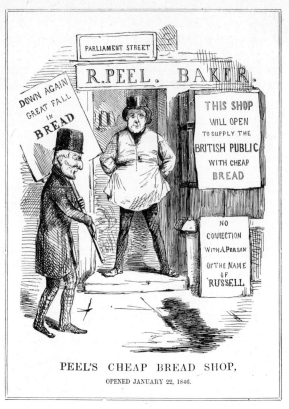

PEEL'S CHEAP BREAD SHOP,
OPENED JANUARY 22, 1846.

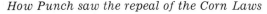

How Punch saw the repeal of the Corn Laws

Hero or traitor? Sir Robert Peel

foreign competition. In Britain, the feeling grew that farmers were being helped at the expense of everyone else.

As the century went on, Britain became more industrialised. The population grew, factories increased their production and merchants made a good living from trade. But some of the manufacturers wanted to abolish the Corn Laws. They believed in Free Trade. They held that the government should not interfere in trading. The Corn Laws made it difficult for foreigners to sell their crops in Britain. However, they also made it difficult for British manufacturers to sell their goods abroad, because the Corn Laws made some foreigners refuse to buy British products.

In 1828 the Corn Law was altered. A sliding scale of charges was brought in. As the price of home grown corn rose, the duty on foreign corn was lowered. For example, if the price of British wheat ever rose to 73 shillings (365p) per quarter, the duty on one quarter of foreign

wheat was only 1 shilling (5p). However, this alteration to the Corn Laws made little difference to the price of a loaf of bread for ordinary people. That remained high.

During the later 1830s there was a depression in British trade. There was great hardship for thousands of people. A movement was started with the aim of abolishing the Corn Laws. It was formed in 1839 and was known as the Anti-Corn Law League. The League had its headquarters in Manchester. That great manufacturing city soon became the centre of the movement for Free Trade. A careful campaign was begun. Pamphlets were printed and sent all over Britain. Letters were written to newspapers. Public meetings were held to discuss the matter. Questions were asked in Parliament.

Two famous leaders of the movement became Whig members of Parliament in the 1840s. They were Richard Cobden and John Bright. Their arguments were listened to carefully.

However, the landowning groups were strongly opposed to them and all that they stood for. The interests of the landowners were mainly represented by the Tory Party.

Sir Robert Peel came to power at the head of a Tory government in 1841. In the next year he introduced a bill which made a small alteration to the Corn Law. The scale of duty to be paid on imported corn fell by 1 shilling (5p) per quarter as the price of British corn rose by 1 shilling (5p) for the same weight. But gradually, Peel himself was becoming convinced that the Corn Laws were harming the nation.

Cobden spoke well in the House of Commons. He went carefully, point by point, through the advantages which Free Trade would bring. At length, Peel saw that he could not honestly answer these arguments. In his own mind he became convinced that the Corn Laws would have to be repealed, that is, abolished. However, as leader of the Tory Party which was mainly opposed to Free Trade, he was in a difficult position. He decided to try and make an effort to change the opinions of his friends. It would have to be a slow and gradual effort. However, an event occurred which altered his plans. In Ireland, the potato crop failed. Many of the inhabitants of that country were faced with rapid starvation. In 1845 there was a poor corn harvest in England. Peel told his colleagues that he intended to repeal the laws. Many of them opposed him, so he resigned in December 1845. But the Whigs could not form a government, so Peel came back to office.

In 1846 he spoke out strongly against the Corn Laws. Some of the Tories supported him, but others could not change their minds. He had great support from his Whig opponents. Since the Reform Bill of 1832, there had been great changes in Parliament, and many new members objected to the Corn Laws. At last, in June of that year, the laws were repealed.

Peel was called a traitor by many Tories. They soon voted against him on another matter and he went out of office. He had split his Party and they did not come back to power for many years. But Free Trade had won a great victory. The old landowning interests had suffered a defeat in Parliament. Britain began a period when her industry and trade led the World.

1846
Irish Famine

POTATO BLIGHT CAUSES TRAGEDY

Hundreds of Irish peasants starve: Failure of potato crop: A nation ruined

The Irish village was quiet. Usually there were groups of people moving about during the morning. There were tasks to be carried out and the villagers worked very hard. Today, however, there was hardly any movement. The few people who came out walked slowly. They looked ill. Their faces were drawn and full of worry as they shuffled along the street. Inside the houses, many men, women and children were lying about. They did not have the energy to get up and walk. Even the animals were still. The village was a place of silence.

The year was 1846 and there was a harsh reason for what was happening. It was a time of hunger. The villagers were desperately short of food. Some of them had not eaten for several days. Their own crops had failed. The same thing had happened in all of the villages in the district. Therefore there was no chance of any food being sent in from nearby areas. The whole countryside was striken by famine.

The food which was so important to the Irish was the potato. For years, it had provided the main diet for most people in Ireland. Mixed with milk or buttermilk, it was a good food for the thousands of families who lived in the countryside. The potato was easy to grow there. The climate provided plenty of rain. From time to time, the labourers had to earth-up the growing potatoes. They were easy to harvest.

The small houses, known as cabins, which were found all over the countryside were surrounded by potato fields. Enough of the vegetable could be grown on one hectare to feed a whole family for a year. The crop also provided food for the animals – cattle, pigs and chicken.

The population of Ireland had grown very rapidly during the early part of the nineteenth century. By 1841 there were well over eight million people living there. Most of them grew their own crops and tended their own animals. That was their life. Few worked for other men. There was hardly any industry. The growing of potatoes was most important to ordinary families. Therefore it was obvious that if any crop failed, there would soon be trouble. This is what happened in Ireland in the 1840's.

The cause of the tragedy was blight. Potato blight is brought by a fungus. The plants suddenly wilt. Their leaves turn black and the potatoes growing in the ground become rotten. Blight had been found in various parts of Europe before 1845. Sometimes it had led to starvation for large numbers of people. But there had never been such a widespread outbreak as the one which occurred in that year.

The interior of a peasant hut during the famine

There was great unhappiness in Ireland when the blight was found there. Many of the poor realised that they were faced with ruin. Potatoes were vital to them. Whole fields of growing crops wilted within a few days. When they were dug, about October, the worst fears were realised. The vegetables became a rotting, smelling mess within a few days. They were useless.

The British Government were soon given warning of what would follow. The food already in the country would soon rise in price. The poorest people would not be able to buy it. Within a few months, that is, about the spring of 1846, there would be widespread famine.

At that time, the Prime Minister was Sir Robert Peel. He was at the point of upsetting his own political party, the Tories, by repealing the Corn Laws. Free Trade would follow. It was hoped that ordinary people would benefit, because prices of food would be lowered. Peel believed that the ideas of Free Trade could be applied to Ireland at once. Businessmen could import and sell all of the food that was needed.

Ireland was part of Great Britain. However, the people of England generally had little idea of the position of many peasants in Ireland. To them, the Irish were very different. They believed that they were a troublesome nation who were simple and unreliable. There were strong religious differences which had led to terrible troubles in the past Most Englishmen were Protestants. Most Irishmen were Roman Catholics. Therefore there was often

Here and There: *Punch recommends emigration*

A scene at Cork, as some Irish emigrate to find a new life

little sympathy for the starving people, even when their conditions were known.

And it was difficult to know exactly how bad the conditions were. Today, newspapers and television bring the news to everyone's attention very quickly. Governments take speedy steps to send help when there is an emergency. But in 1846 there was often a long time before news could be spread. There was no telegraph between England and the remote areas of Ireland.

While some steps were being taken in Ireland, famine swept through the country. The disaster was far greater than most people had imagined. In many areas there was immediate starvation. Some of the villages had no shops. There were poor roads and no swift transport for carrying food. Soon deaths occurred. Men, women and children grew very weak. They could not resist illness.

Thousands had no work. It had been the policy of English governments to allow few industries to develop in Ireland. They did not want them to compete with those in England. Therefore, many men could earn nothing. Although people were starving, supplies of food, especially corn, were shipped out from Irish ports. This was done to encourage the country's trade and bring in wealth. However,

it naturally often led to riots and bloodshed when the hungry saw food being sent away.

The government imported some food. Also, private societies and individuals made great efforts to overcome the famine. But their work was on only a small scale. The famine and its effects went on for a number of years. It is not known exactly how many people died, but the figure must have been about one and a half million.

For thousands of others, there was no future in Ireland. They felt that the English were hated landlords, and overlords who turned them off the land with little warning. Therefore they saved hard to raise a few pounds. Then they could afford the fare to emigrate. Within five years after 1846, about one million people had left Ireland. Many went to settle in North America. The Irish population was given as 8,175,124 in the census of 1841. Ten years later, the figure was 6,552,385. By the early years of the present century it had dropped to 4,390,219.

Those who went to the New World carried bitter memories with them. Those who remained lived in a country which was still troubled by the problems of land ownership, government and religion. The difficulties of Ireland have not been solved today.

1848
The Chartists

RADICAL DEMANDS REJECTED

Demonstration fails: Stern government measures: Petition was a fraud

It was a big demonstration. Thousands of men and women turned up to take part. However, there were not as many as the organisers had hoped. Many others came along to watch. The meeting took place on Kennington Common, in south London on 10th April 1848. This was to have been the greatest gathering ever of Chartists in Great Britain. They were determined to influence Parliament with their political ideas. In their view, they had been treated unfairly for years. The time had come for a change. If necessary, there would have to be a revolution in Britain. This had happened recently in some other European countries. The forces of change were ready for action.

Chartism was a political movement in Britain. The Great Reform Bill of 1832 had given the vote mainly to people of the middle class. However, there were thousands of working class men who felt entitled to vote. They were good, hard working citizens. They believed that they were unfairly treated. They had no vote. Many became Chartists.

They were called Chartists because they supported the People's Charter. This was a list of their aims which had been produced in 1838. There were six points. One was that all men over the age of 21 should be allowed to vote. Another was that all voting should be carried out in secret. Thirdly, Members of Parliament should be paid. Next, a parliament should last for no longer than one year. The fifth was that electoral districts should be roughly equal in size. The last point was that men should not have to own property before they could become Members of Parliament.

In the 1830's and 1840's, groups of these men united. Life sometimes became very difficult, with high prices for food and periods of unemployment. Therefore, they strove hard to make the government listen to their views. For some years the Chartists were a strong force in Britain. Yet by 1848 they had had very little success. Living conditions were beginning to improve. It seemed to some people that Chartism was dying out.

However, in that year there was unrest in a number of European countries. There were revolts against several governments. Therefore, the Chartists decided to hold a monster demonstration in London. When the British government learned what the Chartists were

Chartist demonstration on Kennington Common

A Chartist procession

planning, they were very worried. Such a meeting could easily lead to great trouble; there could be blood-shed. Some people were scared by the thought that revolution might break out, and took steps for the protection of the capital. The Duke of Wellington was put in charge of its defence. Members of the police force were made ready. Troops were warned that they might be needed. Thousands of citizens were sworn in as special constables.

The organisers of the great meeting were members of the Chartist National Convention. Their leader was a remarkable Irish lawyer, Feargus O'Connor. For some years he had played an active part in the movement. He was editor of a Chartist newspaper which he owned, called the *Northern Star*. O'Connor was a Member of Parliament for Nottingham.

The plan was for Chartists to gather from all over Britain. After the monster demonstration had been held on Kennington Common, they would divide into two groups. These would then march into the city. One would cross the Thames over Westminster Bridge, the other

by Blackfriars Bridge. They intended to join up in Trafalgar Square and the Strand. From there, they would march down to Parliament and present a petition to the Speaker of the House of Commons.

For some time beforehand, signatures had been gathered on a petition. It was a document which asked the government to grant the six points of the Charter. The leaders of the movement were very pleased because they said that millions of British people had signed. They had high hopes that their plans would be successful. However, the government were equally determined. Some days before the meeting they announced that not more than ten people could present a petition. Warnings were given against taking part.

The Duke of Wellington was seventy-nine years old. But in spite of his age, many people, especially those who owned property, had great faith in him. He was still 'The Iron Duke', the victor of the Battle of Waterloo. He decided to stop the marchers from crossing the bridges into the capital. Thus they would not be able

An illustration from the 1830s typifying the unrelenting attitude of the Government

Mr Mayne, a Commissioner of Police was waiting for him there.

The Chartist leader walked over. He was told that the meeting could take place. Speeches could be made and resolutions passed. However, there could be no attempt to march on Parliament. That would bring trouble. A few Chartists would be allowed to drive to Westminster with their petition. O'Connor tamely agreed and went back to address his followers. Soon their meeting broke up and all streamed off home. The demonstration was a failure.

The petition was divided out and carried in three cabs to Westminster. It was presented there by O'Connor on the same evening. He said that it contained 5,706,000 signatures. A committee was set up to examine the document. When they gave their report, O'Connor was laughed out of Parliament. They announced that there were only 1,975,496 signatures. Some were written several times over. Other people had signed names, such as 'Duke of Wellington', 'Pug Nose' and 'April 1st'. The Chartist effort had been something of a joke.

Yet in earlier years the movement had been very strong. In 1839 and 1842 there had been greater hardship for people. Petitions were presented to Parliament then. There were outbreaks of violence in parts of the country. But by 1848 the leadership was weak. Conditions of life were improving for many working-class people. Therefore they were not prepared to risk their lives in a revolution.

The Chartists were ahead of their time. It was not until years later that most of their aims were granted. Today, five of their Six Points are part of Britain's laws.

to reach their goal, Parliament.

On this day, there was enormous excitement in London. Processions and crowds gathered in different places. They marched or walked out to Kennington. It is difficult to know exactly how many were there. Several spectators put the numbers at 50,000. There may have been more. Feargus O'Connor and other leaders arrived at the end of the morning. One of the carriages contained five huge bundles of signatures, which made up the petition. As soon as he arrived, a police officer asked O'Connor to go over to the Horns Tavern.

1848
Cholera

DISEASE SPREADS FROM EUROPE

Dreadful cholera plague in England: Many poor people die: Dirt and disease go together

A doctor hurried along a dingy alleyway. In front of him ran a haggard-looking woman. Deep worry showed on her face. Her clothes were dirty and tattered. A filthy shawl was pulled around her shoulders. Now and again, she turned to the doctor, begging him to hurry faster. Their way led through the deepest part of a slum area in London. The paths and alleys were cobbled. Some of them were covered in slime from sewers which had overflowed. One sewer was open and ran past the end of several backyards of houses. There was a strong stench over the whole district.

People's homes were shabby. Some had broken doors and window-frames. In others, the walls were cracked and damp. The district gave the feeling of neglect. The doctor was taken down to a dark basement room. In one corner was a broken-down bed, covered with dirty pieces of cloth. There, a man lay ill. In other parts of the room were six children. They were as filthy and uncared for as their mother. With great care the doctor examined the sick man. Then he turned to the woman, with a solemn face. He told her that her husband was yet another victim of a dreadful illness which was affecting parts of England at that time. She went pale at the news. Her husband had cholera.

The year was 1848. At that time in the Victorian Age the standards of health were low when compared with those of the present day. For centuries, people accepted the fact that death came quickly and easily to many

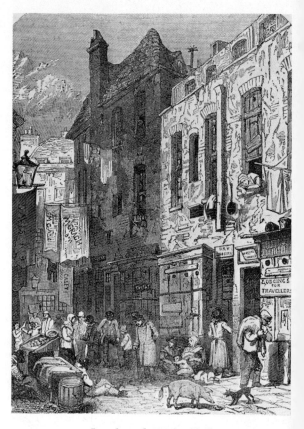

London slums in 1848

families. They did not understand that much disease is spread by dirt and ignorance. Medical knowledge was poor. Therefore little was done to fight against large scale outbreaks of illness.

One of the results of the coming of the Industrial Revolution was a great increase in the amount of building. As the population began to rise quickly, from the middle of the eighteenth century, more homes were required to hold the people. This happened

A great reformer of public health,
Edwin Chadwick

cities, the death-rate was terribly high. Young children up to the age of five years were often the victims. They had less resistance than older people showed.

Cholera is a dreadful disease. It is one of the most severe known to mankind. The illness leads to sickness and stomach upset. Painful cramps affect the victim. After some time comes death. In 1831 the disease was brought to England. By the next year, people in London were affected. Many died. The illness spread rapidly through contaminated water and the dirty, overcrowded living conditions of the time.

A number of men in the nineteenth century became very concerned with public health. One who became famous for his work was Edwin Chadwick, who lived between 1800 and 1890. He was appointed to be Secretary of the Poor Law Commission in 1834 and worked hard for them. Because of his overbearing manner he was not popular with many people. However, he was a driving force. A great deal was achieved through his work.

The Poor Law Commission began to enquire into the causes of illness found in London. In 1842, Chadwick produced a famous *Report on the Sanitary Conditions of the Labouring Population.* He showed that bad living conditions were widespread. One particular thing which he noted was that there were few supplies of clean water. He had an ordered mind. Lists of facts and figures were carefully used to prove his points. He showed that, on an average, rich people lived far longer than poor people. City dwellers died earlier than country folk.

particularly in growing industrial cities. People needed to live near their work. Therefore houses were quickly erected. The working people of the time had few facilities in these buildings. There were no bathrooms or flush lavatories. No hot water systems were available. Usually, several homes shared the use of one outside cold water tap or pump. Rooms were overcrowded when families were large. Systems of drainage did not exist.

It was small wonder when bad illness came. And when it arrived, such illness would soon sweep through a house, or a whole area. There was no way of stopping disease. An epidemic would rapidly affect the inhabitants of a town or city. Illness and death followed closely. Families were large and the birthrate was high. It was quite common for women to produce from eight to twelve children in their lifetimes. However, they became used to losing a number of them through illness. In some areas, especially those in industrial

Some years passed before steps were taken to improve matters. A number of people knew that cleaner buildings and better drainage were needed. However, they objected to being told to provide them. They did not believe that the State or the local authorities should interfere with their lives.

In 1848 there was a further outbreak of cholera in Britain. A great epidemic had started in India and China seven years before. Its trail spread into Europe. The disease was even more severe than the previous outbreak. The first Public Health Act was passed by the

British government in that year. A Board of Health was set up which, however, had few powers. Chadwick resigned from the Poor Law Commission and joined the new Board. But a small start had been made with improving health.

The idea of improving sanitation and health made slow progress. Nevertheless, in 1875 Disraeli's Conservative government passed two very important measures. They helped to raise standards throughout the country. A Public Health Act established a system of sanitary authorities. Their duties were to provide such things as clean water supplies and good drainage. Also, in every area there had to be a medical officer of health and a sanitary inspector. The second measure was the Artisan's Dwelling Act. It allowed local councils to buy up and clear away slum areas. They had the power to bring improved conditions.

By the time of Chadwick's death great advances had been made in public health. Gradually, improved medical knowledge and more care by local authorities led to better living conditions. Yet, compared with the present day, much remained to be done. At the end of the century there were still thousands of cases of illness caused by bad living conditions and poor food.

1850
The Don Pacifico Incident

WARSHIPS SUPPORT BRITISH SUBJECTS

Pam beats the Greeks: British fleet supports our citizens: Some doubts expressed

A politician was making a speech in Parliament. His opponents listened to him with anger. They felt that his actions had harmed Britain. Even some of his colleagues and friends believed that he had gone too far. Yet they all had to admire the way in which he was speaking. He was sure that he had acted wisely and justly. The speech was one of the finest which he had ever made.

The year was 1850 and the politician was the Foreign Secretary, Lord Palmerston. The event which was being discussed had occurred far away from England. Yet, according to Palmerston, it was of vital importance to every Briton. It is known as the Don Pacifico Incident.

Don Pacifico was a Portuguese money-lender who had a house in Athens. He had acted as a consul there. Because he had been born in Gibraltar, he claimed to be a British subject.

It was the custom in Greece for special religious ceremonies to be held every Easter. Greek Orthodox Christians commemorated the Crucifixion and the Resurrection. One of their acts was to burn an effigy of Judas Iscariot, the disciple who had betrayed Jesus. On Easter Sunday, 1847, a member of the famous Jewish banking family of Rothschild was in the city. Out of respect for him, the Greek government would not allow the burning of the effigy to take place. A number of citizens became very angry that their Government had interfered with their rights. They believed that Don Pacifico was partly responsible. He was a Jew and had influenced the Greek authorities. Therefore they attacked and pillaged his house. All of his furniture was destroyed and Pacifico claimed that many other things were burned or broken at the same time.

He lodged a claim against the Greek Government. It was ridiculously high, amounting to £31,500. Of this, £4,900 was for the goods destroyed. The remaining £26,600 was for certain claims which he had against the Portuguese authorities. The vouchers for these, he said, had been destroyed in his house. The value which he placed upon some articles was far too great.

Another person also had a claim against the Greek Government at this time. He was Mr Finlay, an English historian, who had property

Palmerston addressing Parliament

British warships of the period

in Athens. He had received no payment for some of his land which had been taken.

Both men appealed to the British government for help. The Prime Minister of the time was Lord John Russell. His Foreign Secretary was Lord Palmerston. Palmerston was noted for his strong policy towards foreign countries. He was popular with many ordinary people in Britain. 'Old Pam', as he was nicknamed, was always prepared to stand up for the rights of his country. He believed that foreign lands should be made aware that Britain was a great power, equipped with a strong army and navy.

Palmerston had been a Member of Parliament since 1807. From 1846 he had been in his second term of office as Foreign Secretary. This position has always demanded an amount of tact and understanding. However, he showed a lack of these qualities. Palmerston's methods upset Queen Victoria. She took a very keen interest in the affairs of her government. At all times she expected to be consulted before action was taken in matters concerning countries overseas. Palmerston sometimes failed to keep her fully informed. Now and again he took steps before she knew about them. The Queen disliked him and his methods.

In January 1850 the Greek government had not met the claims made against it. Therefore Palmerston sent a squadron of warships to blockade the Greek coasts. He believed that, by interfering with the country's trade, he would force the government to pay what it owed. The ships were under the command of Admiral Sir William Parker. They arrived in position on 1st January. Then Mr Wyse, the British envoy in Athens, again asked for the payment of debts. This was a high-handed action.

The independence of Greece had been established in 1829 by Britain, France and Russia. Therefore Britain had certain duties towards that small country. However, Palmerston did not consult with either of the other two large powers before he sent the fleet. They felt offended. Greece appealed to both Russia and France for help.

At length, in April, an agreement was reached between the British government and France over what should be done. It was agreed that £8,500 should be distributed among the claimants and that Don Pacifico's claim against the Portuguese government should be looked at later. But Palmerston did not tell this to Mr Wyse in Athens. Therefore, the envoy kept pressing the Greeks for payment. At length, the Greek government gave way and agreed to his terms, which were far harsher than those agreed upon by Britain and France.

When the French learned of this, they were angry. They considered that the British had

However, Old Pam was not going to give in easily. On the night of 25–26th June he stood up in the House of Commons to deliver his reply. It was his most famous speech and one of the greatest made during the whole century. He spoke for four and three-quarter hours, right through to the early hours of the morning. Palmerston was a patriot. He believed that every Britisher should be proud of his native land. Also, he was sure that Britain ought to protect every one of her citizens, no matter who they were or where they were living.

He dealt at length with the charges which had been brought against him. His views on what British foreign policy should be were clearly set out. Gradually the cheers grew as members listened to his arguments. Palmerston pointed out that in days of old a Roman citizen would be free from indignity if he said 'Civis Romanus sum' (I am a Roman citizen). Therefore, in the same way, a British citizen should be able to feel that his government would give him protection, no matter where he lived.

When the vote on British policy was taken, the government won by 310 votes to 264. It was a triumph for Palmerston and he became even more popular in the country, but Victoria still did not trust him. She wrote that it was wrong: 'to allow a man in whom she can have no confidence, who has conducted himself in anything but a straightforward and proper manner to herself, to remain in the Foreign Office.'

Nevertheless, he remained popular. His attitude was typical of what was felt by many Britishers at that time towards foreigners.

A photograph of Lord Palmerston in 1860

acted in an underhand way. Therefore they withdrew their ambassador from London. The Russians considered taking a similar step. The British government was in a very difficult position. Palmerston's policy had led them into trouble. A full debate was held in Parliament in the middle of June. Many members spoke out against the Foreign Secretary's high-handed methods. They had given Britain a bad name with other countries who now thought of him as a blustering bully. Palmerston's many opponents saw the opportunity to finish him in Parliament.

1851
The Great Exhibition

A SHOWCASE TO THE WORLD

The Workshop of the World: Britain's lead in industry: Giant display in London

The small crowd of people had come from a village in Yorkshire. Only a few of them had ever visited London before. Some of them had never previously been outside their own county. They looked with amazement at many of the sights. There were such large buildings and so many people and so much noise. They had heard much about the capital and it was even more strange and interesting than they had been told.

Now they were in Hyde Park and in front of them was a building which they had come so far to visit. No wonder they stood open mouthed. It was a giant palace made of iron and glass. The sun glinted on hundreds of windows. Iron girders soared upwards. The park was a beautiful sight. Crowds of visitors flocked across the grass and along the road to the greatest show ever seen in Britain. This was the Great Exhibition of 1851.

The group from Yorkshire joined them. As they came near to the building it loomed high over them. They could see inside through the glass walls. Masses of people were already there and some of the exhibits could be easily seen. They each paid their one shilling (5p) entrance fee and stepped in.

It was like another world: in front was a vast hall, containing lines of sculptures. A fountain stood in the middle of the hall, its waters bubbling and glittering with the colours of the rainbow. Beyond the fountain was a throne which commanded two great avenues. At the left-hand side was a golden cage which contained the world's most famous diamond, the Koh-i-noor. There were other statues set amid tropical plants. Over all was a large elm tree in full leaf which was totally enclosed in the building.

As the visitors wandered round the exhibition, they saw goods from many countries of the world. The western part of the giant building was given over to the products of the United Kingdom and its colonies. The eastern end was reserved for those from foreign lands.

The brilliant architect, Joseph Paxton

Aisles and galleries were carefully divided up into exhibition courts. In these, goods of all kinds were displayed for the crowds to see. They could gaze in wonder at a steam locomotive, or an Eastern tapestry, or delicate glassware. By the end of their visit they felt tired out. They had seen so much yet there were parts of the Exhibition which they had not been able to reach. The building covered a space of 8·5 hectares.

Several other European nations had held giant exhibitions before 1850. There was one in Paris during 1849. A feeling grew in Britain that one should be put on in the United Kingdom. Its main purpose was to show the advances in industry and trade which had been made during the first half of the nineteenth century. The idea was taken to Prince Albert, who was President of the Society of Arts. He turned his mind towards organising it. In 1850, a Royal Commission was set up to arrange the exhibition.

They chose a site in London, in Hyde Park and looked for designs of a suitable building. More than 200 were seen and rejected before one was accepted. This was the work of Joseph Paxton. He was the head gardener and manager of the Duke of Devonshire's estates at Chatsworth. Paxton had designed there a large conservatory, made of iron and glass. He decided to use the same materials in his plan for the exhibition. His first sketch plan was made on a sheet of blotting-paper.

It was an unusual structure. There were more than 3,000 iron columns, varying in height from 5 to 7 metres. More than 2,000 iron girders rested on them. There were 83,600 square metres of glass used, with about 55 kilometres of iron gutters to carry away the rain water. Thousands of square metres of timber floor were laid for spectators to walk on.

The building work was carried out at great speed. This was made easier because it was a prefabricated structure. The parts were made in workshops and factories and brought to the site for assembly. The first column was not erected until 26th September 1850, yet, by December 2,000 workmen were employed in Hyde Park. Soon afterwards, arrangements were made to receive the first exhibits.

Raising the girders of the Crystal Palace

In some quarters there was considerable opposition to the Exhibition. It was feared that foreigners would pour into the country. Mobs of poor people would come to London and perhaps there would be outbursts of violence, even revolution. One of the most fiery opponents was Colonel Sibthorpe. However, the fears were unfounded.

The grand opening ceremony took place on 1st May 1851. Queen Victoria went in a royal procession to Hyde Park. There stood the 'Crystal Palace', with its vast area of glass, enclosing three elm trees. Inside was a special assembly of guests. Prince Albert made a speech, a choir sang and prayers were offered by the Archbishop of Canterbury. Then the royal party toured the exhibits. On the first day alone, about 25,000 people visited the building.

It remained open for 138 days and in that time, more than six million visitors went to

Visitors in the Chinese Section of the Exhibition

the Exhibition. Parties arrived from all parts of Britain. Many travelled by the new train services which were then in operation. Thousands of people came to lodge in London so that they could go to Hyde Park and see wonders from all over the World. Some bought season tickets and visited the Exhibition several times. It remained open until Saturday 11th October and that day more than 50,000 people were present.

The Great Exhibition was a resounding success. Millions of Britishers were given the chance to see the advances made by industry in their land. They saw machinery and industrial products. Britain had become 'The Workshop of the World'. A profit was made which amounted to £150,000. None of the fears which were expressed beforehand were realised.

Later on, Paxton's iron and glass palace was removed from Hyde Park. It was taken to a site at Sydenham, in south London and re-erected there. The building stood and was used until 1936 when a great fire destroyed it.

1852
The Loss of the Birkenhead

TROOP SHIP GOES DOWN

The nation honours the brave: Tragedy and heroism in shipwreck: Horror of sharks

Suddenly and without any warning the ship struck a rock. On deck, members of the crew were thrown from their feet. Below decks, men fell from their hammocks and their belongings were hurled in all directions. There was a grinding crash and the iron hull was ripped open as the vessel lurched. The paddle wheels kept churning away, driving her further on. She listed to starboard and sections of the rigging came crashing down. The swell from the ocean rocked the ship from side to side.

All was dark. The time was 2 am and the soldiers and sailors on board rushed and groped in the blackness. Those down below tried hard to get up to the main deck. A few flailed about as they ran to the ladders. Some were quickly drowned by the sea which poured in through the hole.

In an effort to save the vessel, the captain ordered the engines into reverse. He hoped to back off the rock. Then he could either get his small boats away, or else he could guide his vessel towards the nearby shore. This move, however, doomed the ship. As the paddles thrashed away, the rock tore an even larger hole in the hull. The sea rushed in and soon the engine fires were out. The *Birkenhead* could not be saved.

The date was 26th February 1852. The *Birkenhead* was a troopship carrying soldiers off the coast of South Africa. On board were about 640 people. Almost 500 of these were soldiers, with twenty wives and their children.

The night was fine and cloudless. It was very dark, although millions of stars glittered overhead. The sea was quite calm as the ship drove her way onward. She had two methods of power, though only one was being used at that time. The vessel had two large steam-driven paddle-wheels, and sails also. On that night, the sails were furled and the steam paddles pushed the ship forward.

Below decks, all had been peaceful. Men were asleep in hammocks. A few sat quietly in the darkness as the engines throbbed and the vessel cut through the gentle sea. On deck, sailors carried out their duties. In the bows, were two lookouts. A seaman on the port side was sounding the depth of water. At intervals he swung his lead-weighted rope to measure the depth. All seemed to be well. However, the *Birkenhead* was sailing close to the shore. Her course was just a few kilometres from land. She was too near and tragedy followed.

Soldiers poured up on to the deck. Then they began to act in a way that has made the story of the *Birkenhead* famous in British history. Whilst the ship's commander, Robert Salmond set about trying to save her, the senior officer of the troops mustered his men. He was Major Alexander Seton of the 76th Highlanders. The men lined up quietly although they found it difficult to keep their feet as the sinking boat rolled about.

On deck were some horses. They belonged to a small group of Lancers who were being carried. As the vessel pitched, the animals kicked out dangerously. Therefore it was decided to put them overboard. One by one they were taken to the side and pushed into the sea. At that stage, the people on the ship became aware of a new horror. There were many sharks in those waters. Soon the horses were attacked. Threshing and squealing, a

The ship is sinking

number of them were torn by the giant fish before they could reach the shore.

The soldiers' families were assembled on deck. Then came the order, 'Women and children first'. Some small rowing boats were lowered and quickly filled. The wives and children were pushed and pulled into them. The sailors at the oars rowed from the sinking ship. Gradually the bows sank lower into the water. The stern came up higher and higher. The discipline was excellent as the soldiers were brought further away from the rising water. It was difficult to keep ranks, but they stayed together. Few orders were shouted and the men could see the fate which awaited them. Yet their self-control was superb. The ship next broke in two. Masts and spars came crashing down. The tall funnel fell on to the deck. Men were crushed or knocked overboard by pieces of wood or metal.

As the vessel began to break up, someone gave an order to jump overboard. But Major Seton called out to his troops, asking his men to stand fast. He could see that if the soldiers swam to the small boats, they would swamp them. Then, women and children would be drowned. Therefore he asked them not to leave the *Birkenhead*. Only three men jumped into the sea. The rest stood firm. The vessel broke again. The midships section sank and rested on the bottom until only the topmast showed above the surface. Men clung to it like flies above the sea. Hundreds of others were plunged into the water and had to struggle for their lives. Many could not swim and were soon drowned. Many more were attacked by sharks. Others clung to pieces of floating wreckage. A number struck out for the nearby shore. But there were sharp rocks and patches of seaweed which claimed many victims.

After a long and dangerous time in an open boat the women and children were lucky to be picked up by a passing ship. But altogether, only 193 people were saved. More than 450 were drowned. It was the way in which they died which impressed the Victorians. They liked to hear stories of bravery when the hero or heroine gave up thoughts of safety in order to help others. The story of the *Birkenhead* became the perfect model of how Britishers should act when faced with danger, and writers and artists used it as a topic for their work.

1854
The Charge of the Light Brigade

INSPIRING FEAT OF BRAVERY

The Valley of Death: Glorious cavalry charge: No fear of Russian guns

An officer rode up at high speed to the general. He reined in his horse and saluted. Then he handed over the note which he had been ordered to deliver. The general read it. He looked both puzzled and amazed. It was from his commander, Lord Raglan. The message said that he was to stop the enemy from carrying away the guns. But which guns were meant? The general asked the young officer who had brought the note. Which guns had to be attacked? The messenger merely swept his arm towards the enemy positions. He was almost rude in his answer. He said that the enemy and the guns were there.

A cavalry commander was called forward. He was told to attack the guns. The only guns that he and the general knew of were some enemy batteries more than 2 kilometres away. They were at the end of a long valley. Other batteries were placed on the side of the valley to protect them. The enemy had placed cavalry there as a further guard. Thus, the two senior officers believed that the order which they had been sent was madness. Only a madman would ask them to attack such a position. But the order had been given. They were soldiers and had to obey. Therefore their men were drawn up for battle.

There are some moments in war when enormous demands are made upon soldiers. They are called upon to go into situations of great danger. Often they are expected to put their lives at risk. On some occasions they are faced with almost certain death and only the bravest of them can find courage enough to go ahead towards the enemy. One of the most famous acts of reckless bravery involving British troops occurred during the Crimean War, which was being fought against Russia. They suffered enormous casualties, but never flinched. Their courage has become renowned in British history. The occasion is known as 'The Charge of the Light Brigade'. It happened on Wednesday 25th October 1854.

The Commander-in-Chief who had ordered the note to be sent was Lord Raglan. The general who received it was Lord Lucan. Lucan's brother-in-law was Lord Cardigan and he was in charge of the group of cavalry

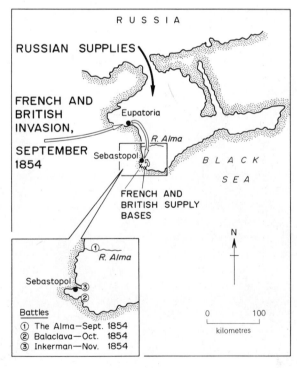

The Crimea, in Southern Russia

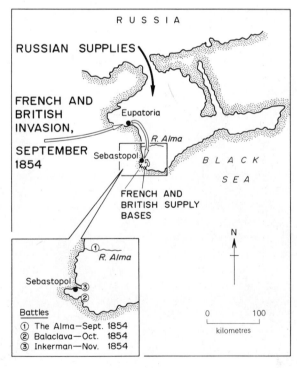
RUSSIA

RUSSIAN SUPPLIES

FRENCH AND BRITISH INVASION, SEPTEMBER 1854

Eupatoria

R. Alma

Sebastopol

FRENCH AND BRITISH SUPPLY BASES

BLACK SEA

N

R. Alma

Sebastopol

Battles
① The Alma—Sept. 1854
② Balaclava—Oct. 1854
③ Inkerman—Nov. 1854

0   100
kilometres

known as the Light Brigade. It was Cardigan who was ordered to lead the charge against the guns. He was angry. The order sounded ridiculous. It was not until later that an explanation was given. The note was intended to refer to some other guns. The whole affair was a mistake.

Cardigan came forward with more than 600 horsemen. Soon after 11 am they moved up in two lines, each of four squadrons. The 17th Lancers and 13th Light Dragoons formed the first line. In the second line were the 4th Light Dragoons and the 11th Hussars. The 8th Hussars were in the rear. As they moved into valley, the officer who had brought the order to attack suddenly rode across the front of the line. Perhaps he was trying to warn them that they were moving towards the wrong guns. No one is sure, because a shell burst killed him at once.

The Commander of the Light Brigade, Lord Cardigan

The Commander in Chief, Lord Raglan

Lord Cardigan then led his men into a charge. When they were about 1,000 metres from the Russian positions, the guns opened fire. A wave of cannon shot, rifle bullets and musket balls crashed into the horsemen. Horses and men were swept over. Men fell and were trampled. Riderless horses ran wildly. The first line suffered heavily. But the survivors did not halt. They were determined to carry out orders. Therefore they pressed home their attack, although they were easy targets for their enemies.

Soon, the Light Brigade reached the guns. They dashed among the gunners, using sabres on them. The artillery was silenced. The horsemen rode on but were faced by two lines of Russian cavalry. They then wheeled round and rode back towards the British lines. Russian troops had moved into the valley behind them, so they had to cut their way through. As they came back, the horsemen were helped by French and British cavalry who attacked the Russian troops.

Then the Light Brigade returned to the British positions. They had suffered terribly.

The Valley of the Shadow of Death, down which the Light Brigade charged

Out of the 600 who had charged, only 195 answered the first roll call. Later, the casualties were found to be 113 killed and 134 wounded. Altogether, 475 horses were killed. It had been an episode of the greatest bravery.

Both friends and foes were amazed at the attack. One French officer said that it was magnificent, but that it was not war! Britain had entered this war in 1854. Throughout the nineteenth century there had been a great deal of mistrust between her and Russia. Britain feared that the Russians were trying to occupy lands belonging to the Turkish Empire. Thus she would be able to threaten British possessions overseas.

By 1853, Russia and Turkey were at war. 1854 saw Britain and France landing troops in the Crimea to help the Turks. But few preparations had been made for the campaign. The commanders were poor. Equipment was lacking. An opportunity to capture the port of Sebastopol was not taken. As the Russians strengthened their defences, they attacked the British positions at Balaclava. At one stage, some British guns being used by Turkish troops were captured by the Russian forces. Those were the guns referred to in the note to Lord Lucan. However, no one bothered to find out exactly what was meant. Therefore the Charge of the Light Brigade took place.

The war went on until 1856. It was a struggle in which more British soldiers were lost from illness than from death in action. The conditions for men at the front were bad. There were shortages of food, tents and medical supplies. Florence Nightingale became famous for her efforts to help wounded soldiers.

There was little glory in the war. However, the bravery of the men in the Light Brigade has been remembered to this day.

1856
The Bessemer Converter

GOOD STEEL AT LOW PRICES

Cheap steel at last: Mr Bessemer's invention: Many new uses

A gang of typical Victorian workmen stood inside their factory. They were dressed in the strong, hard-wearing clothes of the mid nineteenth century. As poor men they were used to performing hours of rough physical work. Life was very hard for them and their large families.

The factory was in Sheffield. It was one of the buildings which had been erected during the Industrial Revolution. Their work was to produce goods made from iron and steel. The products from the factory were sent to many parts of the world. They never lacked work. Demands came in regularly.

Now they stood and looked at a new piece of equipment. Many of them did not understand fully how it worked. However, they were aware that it could make a great difference to their factory's production. They had been told that it would lead to a large increase in production and profits. Therefore they took a deep interest in the large object which stood in front of them. It was called a converter.

The year was 1860. Developments in industry were bringing rapid changes to many parts of Britain. The industrial Revolution was based upon two materials in particular. They were coal and iron. The demand for them was growing. Iron was used for hundreds of purposes. It was to be found in bridges and locomotives, in saucepans and ploughs, in guns and factory machines. From the end of the eighteenth century, the British iron industry grew rapidly in importance.

Steel also was produced, but only in small quantities. The cost of production was high.

The process of making the metal took a long time, therefore it was not widely used. Yet steel had several advantages over iron. It was stronger and lighter. A process was needed to produce the metal cheaply and easily.

This was the problem which confronted the great Victorian inventors and businessmen in the middle of the nineteenth century. The man who found the answer did not know what he was going to achieve. He was not a skilled scientist. But his work provided a method

A successful Victorian inventor and business man, Henry Bessemer

The Bessemer converter at work, 1856

which soon led to the production of cheap steel. His efforts made a headline in his day.

He was named Henry Bessemer and was born in 1813. His father was a type founder. Bessemer had little education in engineering but had an inquiring mind. He became interested in printing and typesetting and introduced some new ideas. They brought him considerable wealth. During the Crimean War (1854–56) he designed a new type of shell which could be fired by artillery. But he discovered that cannons made of cast-iron were not strong enough to take it. Therefore he set out to find a metal which was tougher.

In a number of experiments, Bessemer attempted to remove carbon from molten pig-iron. He did this by working the metal to a very high temperature. It became hot and liquid. Air was blown through it. These early experiments were made in his workshop in London. There he had a cylinder into which the molten iron was run. Then an air blast was let in. The result gave him a form of mild steel which was easily worked.

Bessemer announced his work in 1856 at a scientific meeting. However, there were still obstacles to overcome. One of them came from the fact that there was too much phosphorus

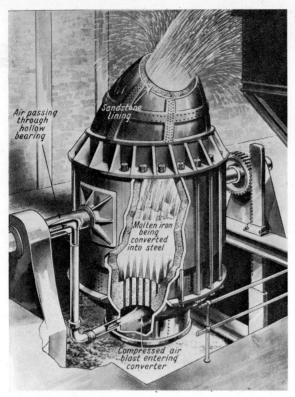

The later, improved converter

parts as wheels, springs and axles. Other firms were allowed to produce Bessemer steel under licence. They constructed such things as rails and plates.

The price of steel was greatly reduced by this new process. But at the same time Bessemer made enormous profits. His process was widely used. In the early 1880s, Britain's railways used even more steel and this demand increased production. During the 1890s, the metal was used for building ships and their engines. Also it was employed in the construction of bridges and buildings.

Although Britain continued to produce large quantities of steel, other countries increased their output. After Sidney Gilchrist Thomas, aided by his cousin, Percy Gilchrist, discovered how to remove phosphorus from iron ore, Germany benefited. Her ores had contained phosphorus. But now good steel could be made from them. On the other side of the Atlantic Ocean, the growing power of the United States was felt by the end of the century. In the 1890s, both Germany and the USA had overtaken British steel production. By 1900, although Britain's works produced 5 million tonnes in a year, the figures for her competitors were 6 million and 10 million tonnes respectively.

Bessemer's invention brought him much wealth. During the 1870s he sold his works at a considerable profit. Others, too, made a great deal of money through his efforts. During that period, many industries expanded. They produced goods which were sold at home and abroad. Britain was indeed 'The Workshop of the World'.

A knighthood was awarded to Bessemer for his work. He was typical of many 'self-made' men of the Victorian Age. They found answers to problems in industry. They worked extremely hard and became rich. These men had tremendous confidence in themselves, firmly believing that they were helping mankind. In later life, Sir Henry Bessemer turned his attention to other inventions. For example, he tried to build a stabiliser for ships. He died, a famous figure, in 1898.

in some of the pig-iron that he used. This made his steel rather brittle. Other men helped him to overcome these problems. Later on, two others introduced new methods to improve the ways of obtaining steel and the quality of the metal. One was Sidney Gilchrist Thomas who found a method of removing phosphorus. The other was Frederick Siemens who used a different method of producing steel.

In 1860 Bessemer devised a new form of converter. It was installed in his factory in Sheffield. This was the object that his workmen looked at with such interest and curiosity.

Bessemer found it difficult to convince iron-masters that his new process would work well. Therefore he had to set up his own works. This he did in Sheffield during 1859. He employed his workmen in producing steel goods for industry. At that time there was a rapid increase in railway building in Britain. Therefore they found a good market for such

1857
The Indian Mutiny

UPRISING AT MEERUT SPREADS

Treacherous attack on our troops: Families in danger in India: Revenge will follow

The British captain pulled up his horse. He was puzzled. Ahead of him lay his army camp. There, he commanded a company of Indian soldiers. All should have been calm and peaceful. The church bells were ringing, calling Europeans to a service. However, he could hear other noises. There was shouting and firing. Suddenly two columns of smoke rose into the air, marking the places where fires had started.

The officer was troubled. After a moment's pause, he galloped on hard. As he reached the camp, a terrible sight met his eyes. In all directions, native soldiers were attacking the British. They had set fire to the section of huts occupied by British soldiers. Bodies were littered in many places. Groups of men were fighting bitterly at one side of the parade square.

The captain galloped towards some of his own soldiers. He knew them well. His shout ordered them to stop and explain what was going on. But instead of answering, they rushed at him and dragged him from his horse. As he struggled to take out his pistol, two of them stabbed him with their bayonets. His last memory must have been of one of his trustworthy corporals taking deliberate aim at him and then firing.

Murders such as this were common on 10th May 1857 at Meerut, a town in India. That day marked the beginning of the first major outbreak of a rebellion which is called the Indian Mutiny. It began as an army mutiny and quickly developed into a war. For more

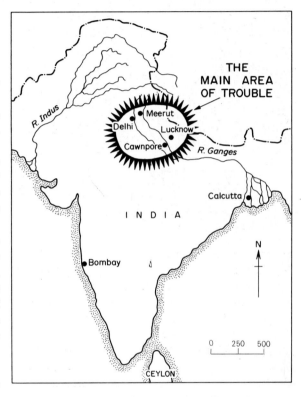

Centres of the Indian Mutiny

than a year, battles were fought in different parts of the country before the rebellion was finally put down.

The British had traded in India since the early seventeenth century. They found that the country offered much to merchants. It contained many goods and materials which were highly prized in Europe. Also, India became a good market for many products made by Europeans. Traders became immensely wealthy and built up huge fortunes. The commerce was controlled by a private

The ruins of Lucknow after the mutiny

company, named the British East India Company.

During the eighteenth century, British and French forces had struggled for power in the country. Each side wished to gain India for its empire. Britain was victorious. Then, over a period of many years, British rule was taken to more and more Indian states. By 1823 it had been established over the whole country. The East India Company had control of all trade until 1813, but after that date others were allowed to take part.

Many Indians were very pleased with British rule. It brought a number of benefits. There was less oppression from some native princes than there had been before. Fairer justice was introduced. In some areas, transport and communications were improved. However, there were other Indians who did not like the British. They believed them to be invaders of their land. They hated the changes that had been brought. Many ways of Indian life had not altered for centuries and it appeared that Britain was interfering with them. The Governor-General between 1848 and 1856 was Lord Dalhousie. He drove on hard with bringing in Western ideas. He began to create a telegraph, canal and railway system.

The British had raised and trained three large armies of native Indian soldiers. They were servants of the East India Company. There were more than 300,000 of them. They had fought for Britain bravely and nobly in several campaigns. The most powerful of them was the Bengal Army. Many of its sepoys, or soldiers, mistrusted the British. Their fears were increased when Lord Dalhousie ordered that the kingdom of Oudh should be taken over by British rule. A large number of sepoys came from Oudh. Stories spread among them about measures that the British were taking. Most were Hindus, believing the cow to be a sacred beast. Rumour said that their cartridges were greased with fat from cows. Rumour hinted that bone-meal was being mixed with their flour.

Therefore, by 1857 a number of causes were all ready to produce trouble. There were small outbreaks before May, but at Meerut on the 10th of that month, it burst into mutiny. When the sepoy regiments had murdered their officers, they opened the prison where some of their number were detained and marched on Delhi. The native regiments there joined them. Europeans were murdered and the rioters declared that British rule had finished.

Revolts occurred in other parts of India. During May and June, the sepoys rose against their European masters in such places as Lucknow, Benares and Cawnpore. At Lucknow, British forces were surrounded in the building and grounds of the Residency. There, they held out for months against heavy attacks until they were relieved. At Cawnpore, after three weeks of defence, the garrison surrendered. The men were then treacherously murdered, while the women and children were slaughtered later.

After the first shocks the British fought back strongly. Many Indian soldiers in other armies remained loyal to them and would not help the mutineers. The civilians did not generally take part in the attacks. The telegraph system, which had been built up enabled news and orders to be passed quickly. The courage and endurance of British soldiers during the campaign was remarkable. In spite of the great heat of summer, they made long marches and then fought in bitter battles. Gradually the mutineers were defeated. Cities were recaptured and loyal units were released

The punishment of mutineers

after withstanding long sieges. Cawnpore and Delhi were retaken, although Lucknow was not finally relieved until the following March.

Great barbarity was used by both sides. The British were particularly angered by the massacre at Cawnpore. The bodies of many innocent women and children had been thrown down a well after they had been murdered. Therefore British soldiers took a terrible revenge. The rebels were hunted down without mercy. Then hundreds of them were put to death as a punishment for what they had done and as a warning to others.

After the Mutiny, the British felt very bitter towards the Indians, especially to those from Bengal. There was a strong feeling that they should suffer for what had happened. However, a wise Governor-General was appointed. He was Lord Canning and was nicknamed 'Clemency' because he realised that such hatred would not solve the country's problems.

The power of government was taken away from the East India Company in 1858. It passed to the Crown. The Company's troops were transferred to the British Army. Britain tried to show greater interest in India, but the memories and bitterness of the Mutiny lasted for many years.

1858
The Great Eastern

GIANT SHIP LAUNCHED

Great ship built: Mr Brunel's giant: A triumph of steam and sail

A man stood high up on the side of the giant ship. He looked a tiny figure, on a kind of platform. The great crowd below grew quieter. The launching was about to take place. She was so large that she was to be slid down sideways into the Thames. A young woman smashed a bottle of champagne against the side. Then she named the vessel – the *Great Eastern.*

The man held two flags. First he waved the white one. At that, the chains and ropes at the bow and stern were released. A great rumble filled the air. She creaked for some minutes then the stern moved slightly. A red flag was waved and huge rams began to push her.

But then came danger. As chains tightened up, one windlass was suddenly sent spinning. The men near it were struck by the whirling wooden bars. Several were hurled high into the air and two were killed. A workman rushed forward and applied a brake. The ship came to a halt – and there she stayed for almost three months. It was an accident in the story of a ship which became noted for her misfortunes.

She was the largest vessel built during the nineteenth century. By 1857 no other ship approaching her size had ever been thought of or planned. No larger ship was to be built for forty-nine years. Yet in that year she continued to grow in the Deptford building yard where she had been laid down several years before. People passed close by to gaze at the monster on the stocks. Scores of workmen clambered over her, fixing timbers, moving iron girders and riveting plates.

Several years before, her designer had had the idea of building a giant ship. His name was Isambard Kingdom Brunel. He was probably the greatest engineer of the century. At that time, Brunel had already made himself famous. He was responsible for the building of much of the Great Western Railway. He also designed docks and bridges. Ships were of particular interest to him. The Victorian Age was an era of coal and iron. Brunel believed in

Isambard Kingdom Brunel, the engineer

iron ships. He had already built the famous *Great Britain*, which was launched in 1843. She was then the World's first ocean-going iron ship, driven by propellers.

The *Great Eastern* was the height of his ambition. He hoped that she would be used on voyages to the East. She was to be so big that she could carry all of the coal needed for the voyage. Other smaller vessels would not be able to compete. Brunel intended that his giant, when in service, would carry some 4,000 passengers.

The ship was laid down at Scott Russell's yard on the Isle of Dogs, Milwall. Thus, Londoners were able to watch her grow. She took years to build. The vessel was nearly 230 metres long and 37 metres wide. She displaced more than 22,000 tonnes. She had five funnels. Her engines turned two giant paddle-wheels and a 24 foot screw propeller. Also, she carried 5,440 square metres of sail on six masts. A special feature of the construction was a double hull, with an inner and an outer shell.

But in spite of her greatness, the ship was a constant worry to Brunel. He drove himself hard at work. For hour after hour he toiled away, designing machinery, studying plans and thinking of ideas. In many ways he was years ahead of his time. He was nicknamed 'The Little Giant', being only 162 centimetres tall. The *Great Eastern* was a wonderful vessel, but she led her creator into money troubles.

The firm that built her went bankrupt. The cost of getting the ship afloat after she had stuck at the launching was enormous. Brunel became ill with worry. At length she was bought by a new company – the Great Ship Company, for £160,000. Its directors decided to use the ship on the North Atlantic route to America. She had not been built or intended for this run.

At long last, in September 1859, she left the

Launching day for the great ship

73

Thames on her maiden voyage. As she moved down the Channel, off Hastings, there was an explosion. A funnel was blown out of the ship by steam pressure. Five sailors were killed. When Brunel learned the news it helped to lead to his death.

Repairs to the ship took some time. Then she was taken round to Holyhead. Late in October, a great storm blew up there. The *Great Eastern* showed the good quality of her construction. She broke away and drifted. Through a night which wrecked many other vessels, her captain kept her afloat.

At length, in June 1860 she left Southampton, bound for New York. It was a remarkable voyage. On board was a crew of more than 400 men. Yet there were only thirty-five fare-paying passengers. The giant engines churned away, driving her across the Atlantic. Twelve days later, she reached New York. There was a tremendous reception waiting for her.

But the *Great Eastern* was never a success as a passenger vessel. Her engines were not really powerful enough for her size. There were many accidents which interrupted voyages. In 1865 she was used as a cable-laying ship. For some time she sailed across the Atlantic, laying a link between Britain and North America. This was a vital step in the spread of communication during the century. Afterwards she was taken on a journey to the East.

The vessel was later kept as a huge, floating show-boat at Liverpool. On board were bands, exhibitions and shooting galleries. It was a sad end for the Great Ship.

Eventually she was sold for £16,000 to a scrap dealer. His men began to break her up on the 1st January 1889. Her copper fittings were sold for £3,000; the plates and rivets brought £25,000. A giant iron ball, raised by a steam engine, was used to burst her apart. As the breakers opened the ship's shell, they found two skeletons inside. The bones were of workmen who had died there, perhaps trapped and sealed in, while the *Great Eastern* was being built. It was the end of the most remarkable vessel seen in the nineteenth century.

1859
Origin of Species

DESCENT FROM THE APE?

New book shocks clergymen: Science v. Religion: Where and when did man begin?

Two men were deep in argument. They were men of wealth and good education. The conversation was taking place in the library of a large country house which one of them owned. Gradually the argument became more heated. It was about a book which lay on the table in front of them. They were disagreeing about what the book claimed. Each of them had read it carefully, because it was so startling. Then they had read some chapters again and again. One of the men had been gradually convinced that what the book said was right. The other was sure that it was wrong.

The year was 1859. The book had not long been published and had come as a bombshell to many learned people in Britain. Its title was *Origin of Species* and the work had been written by Charles Darwin. He had set out to question views about how life had developed on the Earth. In doing so, he had thrown doubt on some people's religious beliefs. And religion was such an important part of life in the Victorian Age that some men were violently angry with Darwin. They wondered why he had dared to attack beliefs and ideas which had been held for centuries.

Darwin had not come to his conclusions quickly. They were the result of years of careful observation, thought and study. In particular, he claimed that different types of living creatures on the Earth had not been created suddenly. Instead, they had been developing over thousands of millions of years. In the struggle for life, some species had not been successful. They had died out. Others, however, remained because they were able to fit in with their surroundings. This was what was known as 'the survival of the fittest'.

The book was not intended to be an attack on Christianity. Darwin simply set out the facts that he believed to be true. And he based his ideas on scientific experiment. He was not content to make a statement without trying to prove it. But, naturally, *Origin of Species* was seen as a book written against religion. Its ideas did not agree with what was written in the Bible. For example, the story of the Creation, in the book of Genesis did not agree with Darwin's points about slow evolution.

Charles Darwin

T. H. Huxley, who supported Darwin's ideas

Therefore the book caused great interest and argument, and its author was soon the centre of attention.

Darwin was born in 1809 at Shrewsbury, where he went to school. Later, he entered Christ's College, Cambridge, and studied medicine. At one time he thought of becoming a clergyman but he was very interested in plants, animals and geology. Therefore he took the opportunity of going on a most important and interesting voyage.

This was a naturalist expedition, made on board H.M.S. *Beagle*. The journey lasted for five years, from 1831–36. It took him to many different parts of the world. For example, he visited the Galapagos Islands, Tahiti and New Zealand. Wherever he went, Darwin made a most careful study of the animal and plant life found there. He was not prepared to accept the usual teachings about how things developed. He liked to put ideas to the test. If possible, he wanted proof before he would believe something. In this he showed a true scientific outlook.

After Darwin returned to Britain he married and settled down to live in Kent. He set up home at the village of Downe. He lived and worked there for the rest of his life. For much of the time he suffered from bad health. However, his work continued. Over the years he read widely. Gradually he gathered together the proof for his beliefs. One of Darwin's friends Alfred Wallace, was also a naturalist. Wallace and Darwin both agreed about the way in which different forms of life had begun. Some of their work was published in 1858. Immediately, it aroused interest. Darwin's main work, the *Origin of Species*, was published in November 1859. It was received eagerly. The whole of the first edition was sold out on the first day!

Then came the arguments. Most scientists of the time were prepared to accept Darwin's case. The man was something of a genius. He had made his points carefully. Proof was given to support what he had said. But many people simply could not believe that what he had written was true. It was felt that he contradicted what the Church taught and Church leaders, archbishops and bishops, argued that Darwin's book was an attack on Christian belief. So, many of them wrote and spoke out boldly against it. One in particular who did this was the Bishop of Oxford, Samuel Wilberforce. He attended a meeting of the British Association and took part in a debate. His main opponent there was T. H. Huxley, a well-known scientist. The views which they spoke in public showed the great differences which existed between many scientists and many churchmen. The Bishop said that Darwin's ideas were wrong and ridiculous. Huxley asked him to offer proof, as Darwin had done.

The argument went on for many years. The whole question was of interest to a large number of people. Whether or not they agreed with Darwin's views, many of them thought deeply.

In spite of his ill-health, Darwin lived on until 1882. Later in his life, he wrote several other books. But none of them caused the kind of stir that had come in 1859. His *Origin of Species* was one of the most important books published during the nineteenth century.

THE LION OF THE SEASON.

ALARMED FLUNKEY. "MR. G G-G-O-O-O-RILLA!"

A Punch cartoon comments on Man's ancestors

1861
The Trent Incident

BRITISH NEUTRALITY MAINTAINED

Risk of war: Americans fire on British flag: Passengers forced to leave our ship

About noon on 8th November 1861, two ships sighted each other in the waters near the West Indies. The vessels, like a number at that time, were driven both by steam engines and by sails. One was a British ship. She was a Royal Mail steamer named the *Trent*. The other was a warship. She belonged to the Northern states of America which were then at war with the Southern states. Her name was the U.S.S. *San Jacinto*.

The American vessel turned towards the *Trent* and steamed rapidly in her direction. As the ships came closer, about 1.15 pm, the *San Jacinto* suddenly fired one of her cannons. A cannon ball flew across the bows of the British vessel and splashed into the sea. It was a warning to stop. Then another gun fired an explosive shell. It burst in front of the *Trent*. The unarmed mail steamer lay at the mercy of the warship. Engines were stopped and both ships hove to.

Some small boats put away from the *San Jacinto*. They carried American marines who boarded the *Trent*. The captain of the British

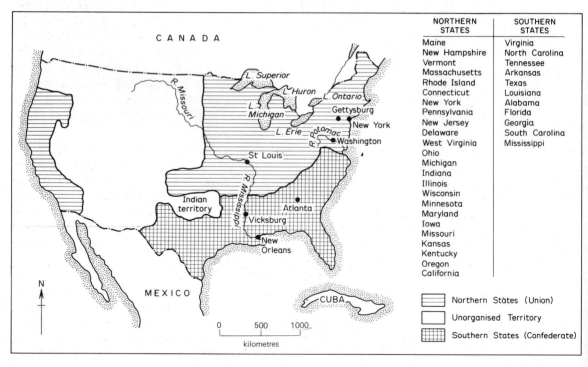

NORTHERN STATES	SOUTHERN STATES
Maine	Virginia
New Hampshire	North Carolina
Vermont	Tennessee
Massachusetts	Arkansas
Rhode Island	Texas
Connecticut	Louisiana
New York	Alabama
Pennsylvania	Florida
New Jersey	Georgia
Delaware	South Carolina
West Virginia	Mississippi
Ohio	
Michigan	
Indiana	
Illinois	
Wisconsin	
Minnesota	
Maryland	
Iowa	
Missouri	
Kansas	
Kentucky	
Oregon	
California	

Northern States (Union)
Unorganised Territory
Southern States (Confederate)

American enemies, the Northern and Southern States

The Trent *(left) stopped by the* San Jacinto

ship was filled with anger. He went up to the lieutenant commanding the boarding party and demanded to know what he was up to. The American officer asked that four passengers should be handed over to him. When they were found, the four men were taken, with their luggage from the *Trent*. The British captain complained bitterly, but it was of no use. After the marines left with their prisoners, the *Trent* was free to go on her way.

She sailed on to England and arrived on 27th November. At once, a report was made to the Admiralty. A number of newspapers also learned of the story. It became immediate headline news. A storm of protest broke out in Britain. It was treated as an outrage. A foreign warship had dared to stop a vessel belonging to the world's greatest naval power. Not content with that, American marines had dared to remove passengers who were going about their lawful business. The British flag had been insulted. Surely, the government were not going to stand by and allow such things to happen!

Why had the incident happened? Who were the four men who had been removed from the Trent? At that time, the American Civil War had been in progress for some months. Troops from the Northern states had already been in action against their fellow-countrymen from the Southern states. A few actions had been fought, but it was obvious that the war might go on for some time.

Therefore the government of the South decided to obtain as much help as possible from other lands. In particular, they believed that certain European countries might help them. The South provided large supplies of cotton to Europe. At that time, Northern ships were blockading their ports and stopping the trade.

Jefferson Davis was President of the Southern states. He appointed two representatives to travel to Europe. James M. Mason was to visit Britain. John Slidell was to sail to France. Two secretaries, George Enstis and James McFarland travelled with them. Their task was to gain help for the South and to

*Prince Albert, whose efforts helped
to keep Britain out of the war*

harm the cause of the North. The men managed to run the blockade of the Southern ports. A steamer took them from Charleston to the West Indies. They boarded the *Trent* at Havana, in Cuba and felt that they were safe. Nothing could now stop them from reaching Europe.

However, they had counted without the determination of Captain Charles Wilkes. He was the commander of the Northern warship, *San Jacinto*. When he received the news that the Southern representatives were at sea, he decided to intercept the *Trent* and remove them. Wilkes considered that he was perfectly entitled to do this. He was thereby stopping his country's enemies.

When he had taken his prisoners, Wilkes returned to the North with them. They were imprisoned. He was treated as a public hero. Newspapers praised him for his courage against the British. At meetings and parades, he was given a wonderful welcome. The leaders of the Southern states were also pleased. They believed that the Northerners had been foolish. By daring to board a British ship, they would surely bring Britain into the war. Jefferson Davis knew that his cause would be helped. The British would never allow such an insult to be offered without taking stern action.

In Britain, the government had to decide on what measures to take. During the war so far they had been strictly neutral and had shown no favour to either side. However, they felt that the North had now gone too far. At the end of November, the Prime Minister, Lord Palmerston, gave orders to the army and navy. About 8,000 troops were sent straight to Canada. Ships of the Fleet were made ready.

A Note was prepared for the Northern government. It was to be sent to Lord Lyons, the British Ambassador in Washington. Then he was to present the message to the Americans. The Note was strongly worded. It demanded the return of the four men taken from the *Trent*. Also, an apology was requested, because of the insult shown to the British flag. The Cabinet agreed on 30th November that the message should be sent. However, before this was done, the Note was sent to Windsor for the Queen to see.

Many people on both sides of the Atlantic believed that there would be war. Public opinion was strong. Both governments appeared to be determined not to give way. Therefore, when the message arrived at Windsor, it was studied very carefully. At that time, the Queen's husband, Prince Albert, was ill. Nevertheless, his sense of duty kept him working. He read the Note and realised that it would almost certainly lead to war. The language used had to be changed, for war would bring tragedy to both countries. Therefore, he sat long into the night, writing. In the morning, tired out, he went to the Queen and showed her the revised Note. The tone was much gentler than in the previous message, but it still asked for the release of the four prisoners and for an apology.

When the British Government saw the alterations suggested by Prince Albert, they agreed with them. The Note was then sent to America. On 26th December the American government decided that their captain's action had been wrong under international law. Therefore they released the prisoners and allowed them to travel to England.

By the time that the news came to London, Prince Albert was dead. He had died from typhoid fever on 14th December. However, his good sense had helped him to keep the country out of a war which would have led to great losses. Britain did not become involved in the American Civil War.

1865
The Murder of Lincoln

WAR'S BITTER LEGACY

American President assassinated: Killed as North triumphs: Tragedy at theatre

All eyes in the theatre were fixed on the actors. The play was interesting and had reached a critical point. Two men and two women sat in a box, overlooking the stage. One of the men was the President of the United States of America. They were carefully watching the play. Suddenly and quietly, the door at the back of the box opened. A man stepped inside, carrying a revolver. The audience did not notice. One of the men in the box turned and saw the intruder. But it was too late to stop him. The stranger fired a shot into the back of the President's head. As the victim slumped forward, the attacker moved to the front of the box. The President's companion attempted to hold him.

In those seconds, the crowd was clapping. The gunman had chosen his moment well. The noise of his shot had been drowned by applause. He attempted to jump over the front of the box, on to the stage, which was some metres below. This action caught the attention of some of the audience. What was going on in the President's box?

The gunman had made careful plans to get away. A horse was waiting nearby, and the man was already wearing spurs. But this led to his undoing. The front of the President's box was decorated with the American flag. As the escaper jumped down, one of his spurs caught in the flag. He pitched forward and fell badly. His ankle was twisted under him. The man staggered to his feet, shouted something and ran off at one side of the stage before the bewildered audience had any idea of what had happened. In a passageway he was confronted by the stage-door keeper, who received a blow in the face from the revolver butt. Then the gunman burst out of a door. Jumping on to the waiting horse, he turned and was away.

Inside the theatre, all was confusion. People looked in shocked surprise when they realised that the President of the United States had been shot. The wounded man was carried out, across the road, to a house on the other side. He was set down on a bed and doctors were called. But they could do nothing. The wound was mortal. His life dragged on for some hours, but he died on the following morning. The news spread like wildfire. President Lincoln had been murdered. The date was 14th April 1865.

Abraham Lincoln was born on 12th February 1809. His family lived in a log-cabin, out in the woodlands of Kentucky. His father had been a carpenter. At a later time he became a farmer. When Lincoln was nine years old, his mother died. His father married again, this time to a widow who already had three children.

The boy had little education, beyond learning to read and write. He helped his father on the land. After the family moved to South Indiana, he worked on ferryboats and as a pig-slaughterer. Sometimes he found employment as a rail-splitter. After he was twenty-one he began to receive more education. He then was employed as a store-keeper, a post-master and a surveyor. He studied law and became a lawyer in 1836. At the same time he became interested in politics.

He married Mary Todd in 1842. She came from a good Kentucky family. Mary was

Lincoln, in civilian clothes, visiting soldiers during the Civil War

ambitious for her husband and pushed him on. Gradually he became better known, both as a lawyer and as a politician. He was a tall man, standing almost 2 metres. His face was rough and craggy and his body was bony. He had an easy-going manner and showed good common-sense. His honest and straightforward approach to life gained people's confidence for him.

Lincoln was a member of the Whig Party in Congress and represented Illinois. By the 1850's he had not made a special mark there. It appeared at one time that he was losing interest in politics. However, a problem arose which was to make him famous. It was the problem of slavery.

For generations, Negro slaves had been used on American plantations. They were carried as ships' cargo from West Africa, where they had been captured by slave traders. When they arrived in the United States, they were sold at public auctions. The Negroes were in demand. The women were used as cooks and as house servants. The men became

labourers, often on cotton plantations. Cotton brought wealth to the Southern states of the Union. Much of the crop was brought by European countries, especially by Britain. The weavers of Lancashire relied on cotton for their living. They wove into it cloth which was sold in many lands.

But an argument arose in the United States over the use of slaves. It grew during the 1850s and came to split the Northern from the Southern states. The South became resentful of the North's growing industrial strength. She feared that Northern politicians were gaining too much power. A strong group of Northerners believed that slavery was wrong and should be abolished. They said that no man should own human beings.

Lincoln was worried. He did not like slavery. However, his great fear was that the Union would split over the matter. The U.S.A. would become two nations, with one half accepting slavery and the other half rejecting it. He was determined that this should not happen. The South must not be allowed to

Murder at the theatre

secede, that is withdraw from the Union.

In the late 1850's, the argument grew hotter. At length, in 1860 there was a Presidential election. Slavery was a main issue. Lincoln stood as candidate for the Republican Party. When the results were announced, it was found that he had won. Soon afterwards, early in 1861, Southern states started to withdraw from the Union. This led to war. The South formed its own Confederacy and chose Jefferson Davis as President. The North was led by Lincoln. He had received no training in military matters and a hard task lay ahead of this untried President.

The Northern states appeared to be stronger. They had a larger population and industries to produce the weapons of war. The Southerners relied mainly on cotton for their wealth. But their fighting spirit was strong. They produced the best military commanders of the war.

Britain did not take sides. Trouble seemed likely over the *Trent* Incident in 1861, but this died down. Generally, people believed that slavery was wrong. Nevertheless, they admired the fighting ability of the Southerners. The great struggle raged for four years. Fortunes swung each way. At length, the greater power of the North brought victory. The cost had been terrible, with 650,000 dead. As the struggle progressed, Lincoln showed his fine qualities as a leader. Near the end it was obvious that his work would be needed to bring the two sides of the nation together again.

In the same week that the Southern armies surrendered, Lincoln decided to visit Ford's Theatre in Washington. He went with his wife and two companions. And there, the tragic murder took place. The killer was later caught and killed. He was John Wilkes Booth, an actor. He sympathised with the South. His action robbed the world of a great man whose work was unfinished.

1866
The Clipper Race

ARIEL AND TAEPING CLOSE TO THE LAST

The great race home: Who was first?: Close contest for tea clippers

A group of people stood high on a cliff. From where they waited, they had a fine view out across the English Channel. Several small sailing boats were making their way along. But all eyes were looking at two ships. They were racing along under full sail. Hundreds of square metres of canvas were spread to take full advantage of the wind. Both vessels sped through the water as they headed eastwards. They were racing towards the River Thames and London. It was not an organised contest, but the crews were aware of what was at stake. There would be fine rewards and much prestige for the winner and great disappointment for the losers.

The ships were clippers. Of all the sailing vessels ever built, clippers were the fastest and the most beautiful. They have been called 'the greyhounds of the seas'. For a period of years in the middle of the nineteenth century they sped over the world's oceans. Their sleek lines drew admiration from all who saw them pass.

By the early years of the nineteenth century there were hundreds of sailing ships afloat.

The starting place – the port of Foochow in China

84

Those that crossed the oceans were heavy and sturdy in design. They were built to be solid so that they could ride through bad weather. Often their lines were heavy. Their job was to carry cargo and a few passengers safely through dangerous seas.

West Indiamen sailed particularly to America from Britain, crossing the Atlantic Ocean. A longer journey lay to the East and East Indiamen traded with that part of the World. They were larger ships because they had to sail over longer distances. Often they carried a few guns as a protection against pirates and enemies.

The trade by sea with the Far East was very profitable. It had gone on for several centuries. Spices, silks and precious stones were among the goods carried. During the eighteenth century tea became a popular drink in England. Therefore, cargoes were brought from China. The ships had a long and slow journey. The route to the East was far longer than it is today. It went from Britain, down the western side of Africa, to the Cape of Good Hope. Then ships sailed up into the Indian Ocean. The voyage covered about 16,000 kilometres to India.

During the first half of the nineteenth century, clippers were built. They were first developed by shipbuilders in the United States of America. These ships often carried less cargo than some of the heavy East Indiamen, but they were much faster. They cut through the water at up to 16 or 17 knots. An American clipper once averaged some 18 knots during one day's sailing. Clippers were used during the Californian gold-rush of 1848–49. They were speedy and successful in travelling from the east to the west coast by way of Cape Horn. [*1 knot=1·852 k.p.h.*]

British companies used clippers. They carried emigrants to Australia after the discovery of gold there in 1851. The main period of these wonderful ships came between 1850 and 1870. Wool was brought from Australia and tea from China. At first, American built vessels were employed. Later, clippers were laid down in British yards.

In their heyday, these 'Queens of the Sea' took part in some famous races. These were

The most famous clipper, the Cutty Sark

Nearly home! Taeping *and* Ariel
race past the Lizard

contests to bring back the first cargo of tea each year from China. There was a good price paid, as well as a reward given by the owners of the ship. At one time, a bonus of about £1 per tonne in addition to the freight charge was given for the first vessel home.

The best remembered Tea Race took place in 1866. In that year, the clippers loaded their cargoes at the Pagoda Anchorage, Foochow. Among those ships were three that had been built by Robert Steele at Greenock, on the River Clyde in Scotland. They were particularly beautiful vessels. One was named the *Ariel*. She was of 852 tonnes and almost 60 metres long. As a 'composite' ship her wooden planking was set on iron beams and frames. The second vessel was the *Taeping* of 767 tonnes, which had been built three years before. The third was the *Serica* of 708 tonnes. All three had the lovely lines of yachts and could race through the oceans at about 15 knots (28 k.p.h.) for long periods.

The three vessels crossed the Foochow Bar together, some fourteen hours behind another clipper, the *Fiery Cross*, which had got away first. They began on 30th May 1866. A day later, the *Taitsing* left. Other clippers followed, but

they were never in the race. These five took part in a hard and close contest. Their captains crowded on as much sail as they dared, to take advantage of the winds. They passed along the coast of Indo-China, then headed for Anjer. From there they turned out into the Indian Ocean. For some time, *Fiery Cross* was in the lead, with *Ariel* second. But after they passed the Cape of Good Hope, *Taeping* moved into first place. *Fiery Cross* lay becalmed for about one day and this cost her the race.

From the Azores there were good westerly winds as the ships sped up towards the English Channel. The race was nearing its end and excitement was rising. On the morning of 5th September, two vessels swept past the Lizard, neck and neck. They were the *Ariel* and the *Taeping*, which had not sighted each other for seventy days. Every metre of sail was crowded on as they ran up the Channel at about 14 knots (26 k.p.h.). The ships dipped and rolled as the sea swept their decks.

As they came to the pilot station at Dungeness, they fired blue lights. At daybreak on the following day, pilots went aboard. The race continued. At the Downs, they were towed up to the Thames by steam tugs. The *Ariel* arrived at the East India Dock at 9 pm, but could not dock because of the tide. The *Taeping* arrived at the London Docks later, but docked before her rival. She had just won the contest. The prize, or premium, was about £500. On the same tide, a little later, *Serica* arrived and berthed at the West India Docks.

But the glory of the clipper did not last. In 1869, the Suez Canal was opened. It made a short cut to the Far East. Because of the lack of fair winds, sailing ships could not make good use of it. However, steamships could. Soon they captured the clippers' trade. Though less beautiful, the steamers were more reliable.

Only one clipper remains from those great days. She is the *Cutty Sark* which was launched in 1869. Now she lies in dry dock in London.

1870
The Franco Prussian War

PARIS BESIEGED

The great surprise: French smashed by the Prussians: The Emperor surrenders

A company of dejected French soldiers shuffled forward. Their heads were hung in shame, because they had just surrendered. One by one they laid their rifles on the ground at the foot of a tree. Many had tattered and torn uniforms. They were hungry and tired. The surrender meant that they would be able to sleep and forget the terrible days through which they had just lived.

In front of them stood their conquerors. They were Prussian soldiers. Several of the Prussians, were making lists of all the weapons which were handed in. Others carefully loaded them on to carts, ready to be taken away. These men made a strong contrast with the French. They were happy and confident. Their uniforms were smart and they moved about with a definite purpose.

The date was 1st September 1870 and the surrender was taking place near Sedan, in France. The town was near the German border. A French army under the command of Marshal Macmahon had just been heavily defeated. The event was a great shock in a war of remarkable surprises. It was the Franco-Prussian War which broke out in July 1870.

Before 1870 Germany did not exist as a separate country. She was a collection of states. Each had its own ruler and its own government. Some states were large and strong; others were quite small. The most powerful was Prussia. In 1866 there was a struggle between two of the states for the leadership of Germany. In a short, hard war Prussia defeated Austria. She showed herself ready to be the leader of a united country.

However, Germany did not emerge as a unified power until after another war had been fought. This was the campaign which began in the late summer of 1870 between France and Prussia.

At that time, France was a very powerful country in Europe. She was led by the Emperor Napoleon III, who was nephew of the great Napoleon I. He had become President of the Second Republic in 1848. Three years later, he seized greater power. Then in 1852 he became Emperor of the Second Empire. Over the next few years, he made his country stronger and more important in Europe. He wanted to restore the greatness of France to what it had been in the days of his uncle's rule.

But during the 1860's the state of Prussia came to rival France. Her leader was Otto von Bismarck. He was determined to unite Germany under the leadership of Prussia. Another of his aims was to make Germany the most powerful nation in Europe. Bismarck was strong and ruthless. He realised that there would have to be war before his hopes could be achieved. However, the Prussian leader was quite prepared for this.

Napoleon III was angry that Prussia's strength grew so rapidly. When she went to war with Austria in 1866 he hoped that the states would fight for a long time. That would help France. However, the war lasted only for seven weeks and then Prussia won. Bismarck organised the German states into the North German Federation. His policy was going forward successfully, step by step.

Therefore trouble grew in Europe. Napoleon looked for a chance to defeat the Prussians. He was losing popularity in France and wanted to do something to show himself as a great leader. Bismarck saw that war with France

Wilhelm I proclaimed Emperor of Germany, at Versailles, in conquered France, on 18th January 1871

was likely and therefore prepared for it. The quarrel came to a head over a matter concerning Spain. The Spanish throne became vacant and was offered to Prince Leopold, a Prussian. Napoleon objected to this, for it could place enemies on both sides of his country. Therefore Leopold withdrew. But Napoleon asked the Prussian Emperor, Wilhelm I, to promise that he would never allow a Prussian to be considered for the Spanish throne again. Wilhelm refused.

When Bismarck received a telegram informing him of what had happened, he saw his chance. He published it. But he made sure that the wording was carefully phrased. Thus it appeared that each side had insulted the other. There was a public outcry from both nations. War loomed close. The French believed that their army was the best in Europe. They felt that the old Napoleonic spirit would bring them a rapid victory. Their troops would soon march to Berlin. Therefore they declared war on 19th July 1870.

However, the French army was really in a poor condition. The men had a fine fighting spirit. But there was little organisation. Soldiers were sent to the eastern frontier. Some went to the wrong places. Others had no equipment. Officers could not locate their men. There was a shortage of maps. Guns lacked ammunition. On the other side, the Prussian general, von Moltke had planned the campaign for years. His men moved in good order. Railways carried them and their equipment to the frontier with France. Every stage of the plan worked with precision.

When the armies came to battle, the Prussians soon showed their quality. Napoleon's troops fought bravely. Infantry and cavalry showed dash and courage. But they were beaten by German efficiency. The Prussian artillery was devastating and smashed great holes in the French lines. Bismarck's generals were superb. The French army was led by Napoleon. He was a sick man. Throughout August his troops suffered defeat after defeat. One force of 173,000 men, under Marshal Bazaine, was besieged in Metz. Another force under Marshal Macmahon marched to their help. However, Macmahon's army was defeated at Sedan and surrendered. The Emperor himself was captured.

Europe was astounded. The Germans soon took Metz and laid siege to Paris, which held out until January 1871. France surrendered.

At the peace conference, the provinces of Alsace and Lorraine were taken from her. She had to pay huge sums of money to the Prussians. France was humiliated. Napoleon III was kept for a time as a prisoner in Germany. Then he came to spend his last days in England. As for Bismarck, he was triumphant. A German Empire was founded and soon became a very powerful nation in the World.

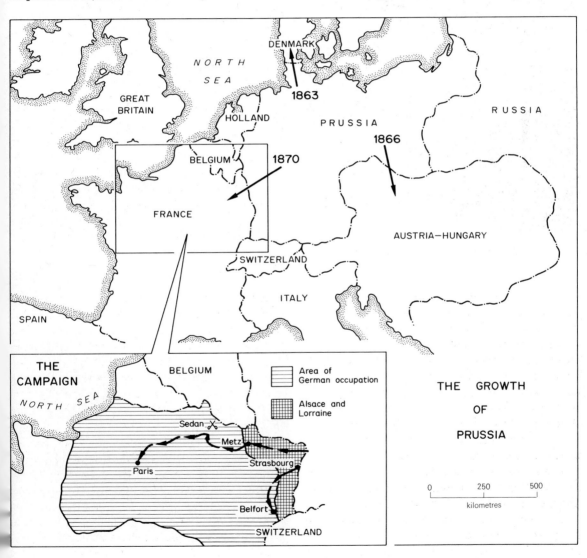

A campaign full of surprises

1870
Forster's Education Act

GOVERNMENT HELP FOR SCHOOLING

Education for all: Mr Forster's important bill: Hundreds of new schools needed

A husband and wife sat talking in the living-room of their home one evening. Their eight children were sleeping. Four of them lay on two old beds in the living-room. The family were poor and the house was overcrowded. They lived in a slum area which was situated in the heart of a large industrial city. The parents were discussing an Act of Parliament which had just been passed. They realised that it would deeply affect the lives of their children. It could alter the way of the whole family. The Act was concerned with education and the year was 1870. The government had passed a Bill which broadened education in Britain. Everyone, boy or girl, would be able to attend school.

Today, education is compulsory for all. From the age of five, all children have to go to school. Schemes are then available for young people to stay at school until they are eighteen or nineteen, if they and their parents wish. It seems hard to imagine a time when there was little education available for children in Britain. Yet that was the situation for many years during Victoria's reign.

There was some education for the children of ordinary people before 1870. It was provided mainly in church schools. The National Society had been established by the Church of England in 1811. Three years later, the Nonconformists set up the British and Foreign Schools Society. Both of these organisations used their money to set up schools. The children of the poor were given a basic education. For some, it was free. Others paid a small sum.

The Victorians had a strong idea of class. There were rich and there were poor. The poor had to be given an education suited to their position in life. Their task was to work long and hard. They had to be taught what their duties were. No great learning was thought to be needed by those who were to work on the land, or as servants, or in factories. The need was for a strong religious education. Also, they could be taught reading and writing.

W. E. Forster

A Board School class in 1890. Could any of these children still be living?

As the century went on, the government took an increasing interest in education. The first grant of money from the State had been made in 1833. The sum of £20,000 was given to the church societies. Just after 1850, the annual figure had risen to about £500,000. By that time, more societies had been founded. A famous one was the Ragged Schools Union. This organisation was strongly supported by Lord Shaftesbury. It set up schools for very poor children and orphans.

During the 1860s it became obvious that a better system of schools was needed in Britain. She was 'The Workshop of the World'. The population had grown rapidly and was still rising, yet thousands could neither read nor write. The face of the country was changing. Industrial towns and cities were spreading quickly over the land. However, some other nations were beginning to develop as industrial rivals to Britain. Therefore her workers needed education.

In 1867 the Second Reform Bill was passed. This Bill gave the vote to about one million more men in Britain. Members of Parliament realised that more education had to be provided. If the nation was to hold its place in the World, the citizens should be educated. There was no sense in giving the vote to working class men who had not been to school. As one M.P. said, 'We must educate our masters.'

Therefore a Bill was prepared for Parliament, by the Liberal Government of Mr Gladstone. The man entrusted with the work was W. E. Forster. He was a Quaker and was MP for Bradford. On 17th February 1870, Forster introduced his Education Bill. He pointed out that it was not intended to do away with existing schools. Instead, they were to be added to in areas where there were no schools. He wanted 'to fill up its gaps at least cost of public money'.

The School Board man finds truants

The 'voluntary schools' run by the Churches were to continue. Bigger government grants were made to them. Where there were no schools, School Boards were to be set up. They were to be chosen by local ratepayers and would offer education to children aged from five to ten years. These were to be paid for partly by government grant and partly from local rates. Parents had to pay up to nine pence (4p) a week for a child's education, according to their income. A big programme of school building was begun.

There was to be 'non-denominational' teaching of religion in Board Schools. That meant that there would not be the teaching of the opinions of any particular Church. In fact, parents were allowed to withdraw their children from lessons in religious instruction, if they wished. A local by-law could be passed to make schooling compulsory. But it was not made compulsory for everyone by Forster's Act.

Many people in Britain were very pleased that the government had helped education. However, there was opposition. Some people thought that religious education should be made compulsory. Others thought that all parents should be forced by law to send their children to school. A number of poor parents did not like a plan which could stop their children from going out to work to earn money. The Bill passed through the Commons on 22nd July. A number of Liberals voted against it. It was a landmark in the story of education. A system was set up from which the schools of the present day have developed.

The schools gave a basic education at primary level. They were expected to teach 'The Three Rs' – reading, writing and arithmetic. Classes were large and the buildings were often grim and gaunt. Compared with many schools of the present day they were forbidding places. But a step forward had been taken. The mass of the population could now be given some education. In particular, girls were given opportunities of learning, which many had not had before.

In 1880, school attendance was made compulsory, up to the age of ten. Eleven years later, elementary education became free. By that time a new need was coming to light. This was for more secondary education in Britain.

1870
The Death of Dickens

WESTMINSTER BURIAL FOR PEOPLE'S NOVELIST

Death of a great writer: He gave pleasure to millions: The nation mourns Charles Dickens

The nineteenth century produced many great men whose names are still remembered to the present day. There were soldiers and statesmen, engineers and inventors. But one of the most famous of all Victorians was a writer. He was born in 1812. His death in 1870 marked the end of a remarkable career. By that time, his books had been read by hundreds of thousands

The famous writer at work. Notice his pen.

of people. They are still widely read at the present time. The writer's name was Charles Dickens.

His father was a clerk in the Navy Pay Office. Charles was the second child of eight in the family and was born at Portsmouth. As a boy, Dickens lived at Chatham, then in London. His parents were often in debt and at length, in 1824 his father was sent to prison. This was the Marshelsea Prison for debtors. Mrs Dickens and the young children went there as well. Charles went to Camden Town and began work in a blacking factory. His wage was 6 shillings (30p) a week.

After his father's release from prison, Charles returned to school. At the age of fifteen he found employment in a lawyer's office as a junior clerk. After a time he gave this up and then became a reporter. His work took him sometimes to the House of Commons and sometimes to political meetings in different parts of the country.

Dickens was a keen observer of the people he met. He came into contact with all types, good and bad, poor and rich. He had the great skill of being able to describe them in writing. Soon he began to send short articles to magazines. The first was published by the *Monthly Magazine* in 1833. Then he wrote several sketches, using the pen-name, Boz. In 1836 he began to publish *The Pickwick Papers* in serial form. They became an enormous success. Soon Dickens became well-known to thousands of people who read his stories with a growing interest.

Over the next few years, he worked extremely hard. Several books were produced which have become very well known in the

THE EMPTY CHAIR.

After his death. Some of Dickens characters are shown around his desk

English language: *Oliver Twist* was written between 1837–39, *Nicholas Nickleby* came out from 1838–39. After this came *The Old Curiosity Shop* (1840–41) and *Barnaby Rudge* (1841).

Dickens had a special skill in writing. In his life he watched people carefully. Then, when he had learned their ways, he wrote about them in his stories. His characters were based upon people he had met and talked with. He was so skilful in writing about them that many of these imaginary characters are still well known today.

It was part of Dickens' plan to show many of the evils of his time. He himself had known hardship when young. The coming of the Industrial Revolution brought great hardships to many poor people. Therefore he brought into his work many characters who showed that side of life. In this way he was able to draw attention to many matters which needed to be improved.

For example, there were a number of private schools where boys were badly treated. Thus, he wrote of Mr Wackford Squeers and Dotheboys Hall, in *Nicholas Nickleby*. The workhouses of the time were often gaunt and forbidding places. Thus he produced Oliver and Mr Bumble in *Oliver Twist*. The same book showed something of criminal life when it dealt with Fagin and Bill Sikes.

In the twenty years from 1841 to 1861, Dickens wrote more books. *Martin Chuzzlewit*, *David Copperfield*, *A Tale of Two Cities* and *Great Expectations* are among the best known of them. He worked extremely hard to produce these works, which were eagerly awaited by his readers.

A great deal about the life of the nineteenth century can be learned from Dickens' books. He gave good descriptions of debtors' prisons and elections, of law courts and slums. The long accounts of his famous characters help readers to know how people spoke and thought and lived at that time, when many changes were taking place as industry expanded and cities grew. The writer's pen was able to show how these changes affected the ordinary people of the age.

Although Dickens found much fame, his personal life was often unhappy. In 1836, he had married Catherine Hogarth, and they had a family. But later they separated and lived apart. Dickens travelled abroad, where his works were read and liked. He visited America and several countries in Europe. Always he wrote about his travels. Not only did he write novels, but also produced magazines. For a short time he was the first editor of the *Daily News*. Later, he began to give public readings of his works. At first this was done to help charity. But from 1858 they were given as part of his work to earn income. Crowds of people would pay to go to halls where the famous author would read some of his works to them.

This gave Dickens the opportunity to act in front of large public audiences. He had the power to draw laughter or tears from them. Thus his writings became even more widely known. However, the strain of travelling and speaking put a heavy burden on the famous man. His health had not been good for some years. Gradually, it grew worse, although he refused to stop or ease up his work.

By the summer of 1870, he was very ill. He lived at a house named Gad's Hill, near Rochester in Kent. It was a house that Dickens had seen and admired when he was a boy. On 8th June he spent his day there, writing. In the evening, he complained of feeling unwell. Suddenly he collapsed. He was laid on a sofa in the dining room. Members of his family and various friends came to be at his bedside, but the end drew near.

They sat with him throughout the night, but he died about six o'clock the following morning. Five days later he was buried in Poet's Corner, Westminster Abbey. The Victorians mourned their best known writer. He had given hours of happiness to thousands.

1873
The Death of Livingstone

AFRICA'S MISSIONARY LAID TO REST

Dr Livingstone dies in darkest Africa: A brave Christian explorer: Loved by Africans

The British explorer was very ill. Bouts of fever had left him weak. The Africans who travelled with him were devoted to the man who had travelled so far in their continent. However, they were very worried about his condition. He was a man of great determination and would not give up. He would not rest in spite of the fact that he was far from well.

At length, his body failed. At the end of April, 1873 he was in camp to the south-east of Lake Bangweolo. The camp was at a place named Chitambo. In the early morning of 1st May 1873, one of the native servants went to his tent. He found the explorer, dead, kneeling by his bed in an attitude of prayer.

The servants were upset. The explorer, David Livingstone, had been like a father to them. They had walked hundreds of kilometres with him and had met great dangers. Together they had overcome many obstacles. Now the journeys were finished. Some of them decided that the explorer's body should be taken back to the land of the white man. Therefore they marked the place where he had died. They took his body and prepared it for the long journey ahead by embalming. His heart was taken out and buried in Africa. His remains were sewn up in a covering of bark. Then began the long journey back to the coast.

Livingstone's servants were very loyal. In spite of the difficulties facing them, they refused to abandon their task. At length they arrived, after a journey which lasted about nine months. The body was handed over. It was brought back to Britain by ship. The explorer was already famous for what he had achieved. Therefore the Government decided that a memorial service should be held for him and his remains buried in Westminster Abbey. Such a burial was reserved for the greatest in the land. On 18th April 1874 the ceremony took place. It was held in totally different surroundings from those that Livingstone had travelled through for so many years. His life's work had been given in Africa.

Until the later part of the nineteenth century, Africa was known as 'The Dark

David Livingstone

Continent' to Europeans. Its coastline had been known for centuries. Since the end of the fifteenth century, sailors had made their way southwards, round the Cape of Good Hope, on their way to India, and the Far East. But vast stretches of land inside the continent had not been explored. A few brave travellers had made journeys into parts of Africa, but much remained to be found.

David Livingstone was born on 19th March 1813 at Blantyre, in Scotland. He came from a poor family and when only ten years of age was sent to work in a cotton factory. The work was very hard and lasted for long hours. But the boy wished to do better in life. He knew that education was needed before progress could be made. Therefore he began to study at home, at evening school and even in spare moments at the factory. Later, he studied in the winter and returned to the factory in the summer.

Livingstone trained to be a doctor. At the same time, he was a very religious man and wished to spread Christianity. Therefore he decided to become a medical missionary. At one time he hoped to go to the Far East and work there. However, in 1840 he was sent to Africa, as there was a war in China. He worked for the London Missionary Society.

After landing at Capetown, he moved north to Kuruman and stayed there working at a mission station for some years. He met Mary Moffatt, a missionary's daughter and married her on 2nd January 1845. Both were serious minded and devoted to the cause of converting Africans to Christianity.

Livingstone gradually became convinced that he would have to carry out missionary work by exploring. The Christian message could be taken to tribes deep in The Dark Continent. At the same time, much would be learned about the geography of vast areas where Europeans had never been. Thus the main work of his life began.

He made a great journey between 1852 and 1856. It took him from Cape Town, northwards to Linyante. Then he travelled on towards the north-west, coming to the Zambesi River and finally reaching the coast at Loanda. With his loyal followers he passed through great

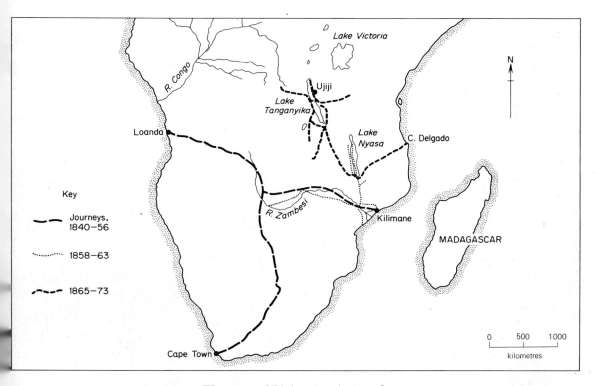

The area of Livingstone's travels

97

Livingstone's funeral in Westminster Abbey

difficulties and dangers. Livingstone refused to return by sea, but went back to Linyante. From there he struck eastwards across Africa to the mouth of the Zambesi. On the way, he came to a great waterfall which he named the Victoria Falls, in honour of the Queen. The journey did not end until May 1856.

He returned to Britain for just over a year and was a centre of attention. Thousands of people had learned of his achievements. He published a book which told of his adventures. Then Livingstone returned to Africa in 1858.

From then until 1864 he carried out another series of journeys. They showed how some areas could be used for white settlers. His travels took him from the Zambesi Basin to Lake Nyasa. At that time he fought strongly against the slave-trade which he found in a number of places. Portuguese and Arab traders dealt freely in negro slaves and Livingstone tried to stamp out the business. A personal tragedy came to him in 1862 when his wife died, but he continued with his travels

and work. He later sailed to India, then returned to Britain.

Livingstone's last period in Africa lasted from 1865 to 1873. He went further north than on previous journeys but met great difficulties. Some of his porters left him and he suffered from bad health. In Britain, before the days of easy communication, little was known of his movements. Therefore an American, named Henry Stanley set out on an expedition to find him. They met at the village of Ujiji, on the shores of Lake Tanganyika. Stanley stayed with him for a few months, but Livingstone refused his offer to return to Britain.

Before long, the explorer moved on, growing weaker all the time. Then came his death. He had carried the message of Christianity to thousands who had not known it before. He had shown the British that parts of Africa would be suitable for settlement and trade. His work helped to lead to important changes in the continent by the end of the century.

1875
The Suez Canal Shares

SHREWD INVESTMENT BY DISRAELI?

Britain buys Suez shares: Waste of money or good investment?: Importance to the Empire

A group of rich businessmen sat back in a first-class railway compartment. They were travelling to London on business for their firms, which dealt in trade with the Far East. As the steam train sped along through the English countryside, they were discussing affairs in a distant part of the World. They were talking about Egypt.

Their newspapers were strewn on the seats. Anyone reading the important news in them would realise why that country was under discussion. A long and detailed report showed that Britain had just taken a keen interest in Egypt. The Government had just bought a large number of shares in the Suez Canal Company. It would now be necessary to watch affairs there carefully.

The men in the train were talking heatedly about this matter. Some of them thought that the Government had taken a wise step. The buying of the shares would bring wealth to Britain. Others believed that the money had been wasted. It meant that Britain now had greater burdens overseas than ever before. She would become involved in the affairs of other lands and it would prove to be costly.

The year was 1875. The Suez Canal had been opened six years earlier. Men in Europe had hoped for a short cut to the East for many years. The old route for centuries has passed around the Cape of Good Hope, at the southern tip of Africa. The voyage to India had been long. However, a Frenchman, Ferdinand de Lesseps, planned a shorter way. He lived for many years in Egypt. It was

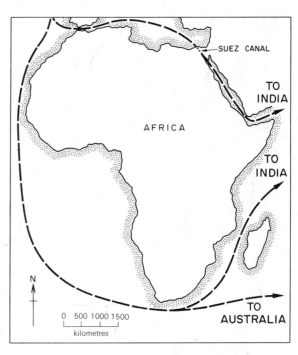

The new canal provided a short route to parts of Britain's distant Empire

obvious to him that if a canal could be built which would link the Mediterranean with the Red Sea ships would be able to sail far more quickly to the East.

The work of construction was completed in 1869. Altogether the Canal stretched for about 160 kilometres. The money to pay for it was obtained by selling shares. A number of people, especially French businessmen, bought them. The Suez Canal Company was set up to run everyday affairs. Just less than half of the shares were held by the ruler of Egypt. He obviously had an interest in a waterway which passed through his country. His title was the Khedive and his name was Ismail.

However, he was not careful in money matters. Several times he ran into debt. In 1870 he had tried to raise some money quickly. Then he offered to sell his shares to the British government. He even suggested that they should buy up the whole Company. At that time, the Company was not having a very successful time. The Foreign Office in London would not accept the offer.

In November 1875, the Khedive again wanted to sell his shares. The news that they were coming on the market was given to the Foreign Office by a British journalist. His name was Frederick Greenwood. When he heard the information, he thought that the government might be interested. Once again, the Foreign Office were not. But the news came to the Prime Minister and he showed an immediate interest.

The Prime Minister was Benjamin Disraeli. He was one of the most remarkable politicians ever seen in Britain. Born in 1804, he came from a Jewish family that had become Christian. His entry to Parliament, as a Tory, was made in 1837. Over the following years he made a name for himself as a brilliant debater and writer. Disraeli was Prime Minister for the first time in 1868. In 1874 he became Prime Minister for the second time. He became very interested in foreign affairs and happenings in the British Empire.

Therefore, when the chance came, in 1875, to buy some shares in the Suez Canal Company, he took it. Already, about eight ships out of each ten using the Canal were British. It lay at a vital part of the route to India. That country was a most important part of Britain's Empire, providing a source of great wealth. The new route to the East was vital to British interests.

Disraeli wanted to act quickly. There was not time to call all of his colleagues together

Benjamin Disraeli,
the Prime Minister who bought the shares

"MOSÉ IN EGITTO!!!"

A contemporary cartoon, linking Disraeli's
interest in the shares with his Jewish origin?

British troopship passing through the canal on its way to India

and ask their opinions. Therefore he decided to borrow the money privately. He went to see a friend of his, Rothschild. The Rothschilds were a company of Jewish bankers who had lived in Britain for some time.

The request was unusual. It was an enormous sum which was involved. Disraeli asked for the loan of £4 million. Rothschild sat back, weighing up the arguments for and against lending the money. At length he agreed. Disraeli knew that his action had been unusual. He realised therefore that his opponents in Parliament would blame him for taking such a step. This they did. Gladstone, the Liberal leader accused him of wasting the country's money. He said that the shares were worth nothing. But at length, the government agreed with what had been done.

The Prime Minister wrote to the Queen, when he had bought the shares – 'It is just settled: you have it, madam.' She had a great liking for Disraeli, who charmed her with speech and actions. Owning the shares caused

Britain to give more attention to the Middle East. It was now in her interest to make sure that friendly governments were in power there. The Suez Canal soon became 'the jugular vein of the British Empire'. Any unfriendly force could do immense harm to trade.

Therefore Britain began to interfere in Egypt. With France, who also had an interest in the Canal, she removed the Khedive Ismail from power. His son, Tewfik, was put in his place. However, the country's finances continued to weaken. At length, there was a rebellion against British and French rule, led by an Egyptian colonel, Arabi Pasha.

In 1882 a British military force landed. There was a battle at Tel-El-Kebir at which the Egyptians were defeated. Britain then gained more power in the country by sending an envoy, Lord Cromer, who for many years helped to control the nation's affairs. Britain's interest in the Suez Canal lasted until 1956, when the Egyptians took over the Canal.

1879
Rorke's Drift

OUR TROOPS WITHSTAND ZULU ASSAULT

A brave fight: Zulu hordes driven off: Heroic defence of tiny outpost

The group of buildings known as Rorke's Drift stood a little way inside the border between Zululand and Natal. James Rorke, a farmer, had settled there in 1849. A long, low farmhouse had been built, with a verandah along one side. Some outbuildings were also erected. Near the site ran the Buffalo River and at this point was a ford or 'drift'. The small and lonely spot became the scene of a violent and bloodthirsty battle which occurred during the Zulu War. In the nineteenth century the Zulus became a great warrior race in southern Africa. The young men were noted for their skill and bravery in fighting. They conquered several other native tribes which lived near them.

The Boers in South Africa came into contact with them. As these farmers of Dutch descent moved northwards away from the area of the Cape of Good Hope, there were several conflicts. The Boers wanted land for settlement and farming. The Zulus believed that they were intruders. By the late 1870s, the British were taking a great interest in Zululand. It was an age of Imperialism when a number of territories were being taken into the Empire. In 1877 Britain had occupied the Boer colony of Transvaal. She did so to protect the inhabitants from the Zulus on their frontiers.

The Zulu king had power of life and death over his people. His name was Cetewayo. For some time there had been trouble between his warriors and the inhabitants of the Transvaal. There were a number of squabbles and arguments along the border. White missionaries had been sent into Zululand in order to con-vert its people to Christianity, but some were driven out.

In December 1878, a note was sent to Cetewayo by the British authorities. It ordered him to stop his warriors from carrying out raids. Also he was asked to accept a British Resident – a political adviser – in his country. He was given thirty days in which to agree. A small British army had been made ready. It was prepared to fight the kind of campaign which had become quite common in the nineteenth century. This was a small war against native forces. Because of their training and superior equipment, British forces almost always won.

As Cetewayo did not agree to the note, war was declared on 11th January 1879. British troops soon advanced into Zululand from the state of Natal. One column crossed the river at Rorke's Drift and marched on. That night, the troops camped below a small mountain called Isandlwana. The next day, the 22nd January, while a detachment of soldiers were out of camp, the Zulus made an attack. The Zulu force, called an impi, consisted of about 20,000 men. It fell upon the troops in the camp and massacred them. A large force of Zulus by-passed the battlefield and swept straight on to Rorke's Drift.

A small detachment of British soldiers was there, including a number of sick men. They were commanded by two young officers. One was Lieutenant Chard and the other was Lieutenant Bromhead. Short notice was given of the coming attack. It came from a horseman who had escaped from the battlefield. At once, they built barricades of mealie bags and biscuit boxes. Even the sick men had to fight. Altogether, there were 141 men there. The

At Isandlwhana the Zulus pour in to the attack

soldiers were dressed in white helmets, red coats and black trousers.

They were packed into a small space but had plenty of ammunition. The Zulus had a few rifles but relied mainly on their assegais, which were sharp stabbing spears. The soldiers knew that they were fighting for their lives. No prisoners would be taken. Therefore the contest was very bitter.

The Zulus arrived and poured straight into the attack. Volleys of rifle fire crashed out. Rifles had to be reloaded after each shot, but in skilled hands they were deadly weapons. The large hide shields carried by the natives were no defence against bullets. The Zulu warriors were known to be the fiercest in southern Africa. In their hundreds they swarmed around the little outpost, hurling themselves again and again towards its walls. As they rushed forward, they screamed with terrible yells. Their bravery and endurance were a marvel to friends and foes alike.

They were confident that they were going to gain another victory. There were less than 150 defenders in the small cluster of buildings. They were trying to hold off the mighty power of 4,000 Zulu warriors. Surely it would not be long before the wave of attackers swept over the buildings. The men inside would be quickly dragged out and stabbed to death. Then the warriors would return to their king. They could report that his invading enemies had been overthrown.

However, the Zulus did not realise how determined the defenders were. Therefore the attacks were met with searing volleys of rifle fire from behind walls, doors and windows. Fierce hand-to-hand battles took place. Bayonets clashed with assegais and men wrestled in the dust. As night fell, the fighting went on. The straw roof of one building was set alight and men struggled for life in the glow of the fires. Soon the Zulu dead were piled high round the defences. And as midnight came, the soldiers defending the post were still holding on. They were tired but unbeaten. In the early hours, the Zulus retired unable to capture the place.

The scene next morning as relief arrives

The toughness and determination of the defenders won the fight. Fifteen of them were killed and twelve wounded. As day dawned, about 400 dead Zulus were found around the house. Altogether, eleven men received the Victoria Cross for their bravery in the action. They included Chard and Bromhead. The regiment later became the South Wales Borderers.

The war continued. More British troops were sent. Later in the year an army advanced carefully to Cetewayo's chief kraal, or village, at Ulundi. There, in a very bloodthirsty battle, the Zulus hurled themselves continually at the redcoats. The natives were cut down in their hundreds by accurate rifle fire. Another campaign of Empire had been won.

1879
The Tay Bridge Disaster

LARGE NUMBER FEARED DEAD

Scottish railway bridge collapses: Train plunges into river: Who was to blame?

The Victorian Age was famous for the great works of engineering skill which were carried out in Britain. The Industrial Revolution led to rapid changes in methods of production, construction and transport. These were seen particularly in the ways that people used to travel about. One of the most important of these changes was the coming of the railway.

In the years after 1830, railway building took place on an enormous scale. The Liverpool and Manchester Railway was soon a great success. George Stephenson's pioneer work was followed by the efforts of others. Within a few years lines were laid down to link many parts of Great Britain. By 1850, more than 9,600 kilometres of railway were in use. This figure had increased to 21,600 kilometres by 1870. It stood at more than 32,000 kilometres by the end of the century.

Travel was greatly speeded up. Never before had it been possible for so many people to be able to move about the country so quickly. It became possible to visit towns and cities hundreds of kilometres away. Journeys which had once taken days, or even weeks, could now be made in a number of hours. Goods, too, could be easily carried. Therefore the nation's trade grew larger. Iron goods, coal, clothing, food and letters are examples of the articles which were sent by train. Other industries expanded as the railways needed their products.

Some towns grew in importance when the railway came to them. Crewe and Swindon, for example, became large railway centres. Also, people could now travel swiftly to holiday areas. Therefore seaside places grew in size. Such towns as Blackpool, Brighton and Margate became better known. An important event in the story of the railways was the coming of cheap steel. During the 1860s and 1870s it was used increasingly in the construction of rails, locomotives and bridges.

British railways became famous in many lands. The 'iron road' stretched out over

Sir Thomas Bouch's bridge. Notice the section of 'high girders'

thousands of kilometres in foreign countries. The work of laying and building railways brought wealth to British engineers, businessmen and workers. Within Britain, the great cities were soon linked by lines. It became a matter of hours to travel from Bristol to London, or Liverpool to Birmingham. However, the network of rails came more slowly to some areas. These were places where there were few large centres of population. Or they were places where the countryside was rugged and difficult to cross.

The north of Scotland was such an area. On the eastern side of that country, the North British Railway had its line. It ran up from Edinburgh to Dundee and then on to Aberdeen. One great obstacle to progress was the Firth of Tay. There, passengers had to cross an area of water. In the early 1870s they had to make this short journey in a ferryboat, joining another train on the further side.

To make travel easier, the owners of the railway decided to build a bridge across the Firth. They called in a famous bridge designer of the Victorian Age. He was Thomas Bouch. He was faced with a great challenge, but all people involved had confidence in his work. A contract was signed in 1871 and the work went on for seven years. Hundreds of workmen laboured to build brick piers, erect iron girders and pour in tonnes of concrete. As the work grew, people looked in wonder at the monster bridge. It was, at that time, the longest in the World. Bouch was proud of his achievement.

Out in the middle of the Firth, the giant bridge rose to a section of high girders. These covered a length of over 1,000 metres. At their greatest height they were almost 27 metres above water level, so that ships could pass underneath. Praise was heaped upon Bouch for his work. In a time of British engineering pride, he had produced one of the wonders of the age. Soon after the bridge was opened in 1878, the Queen herself crossed it. She honoured the designer with a knighthood. Sir Thomas Bouch was at the height of his powers. It appeared that man had conquered a large natural barrier.

After the tragedy divers search for the remains

The second bridge. Notice the old pillars just to the right

However, some people had doubts. In that part of Scotland, great storms could blow. Winds and waves of immense power rushed into the Firth of Tay. Local inhabitants wondered what would happen to the bridge when winter came. It had been tested in good weather. The massive iron struts and bars and the brick piers seemed safe then. Yet no one could foresee the huge tragedy which was coming. On the evening of Sunday 28th December 1879 a train approached from the south. It was carrying passengers towards Dundee. A great storm was blowing at the time. At about seven o'clock, the train came to the signal-box at the beginning of the bridge. The signalman left his box and went down to speak to the driver.

Then the train rumbled on to the bridge. The signalman made his way back to the box as the gale howled around him. He stood, with another man, and watched the lights of the train disappear into the distance. Sparks could be seen as the train moved across. Suddenly there was a bright flash, then blackness. The signalman was worried. He tried to telegraph to the other side of the bridge, but the line was broken. When he went outside with his companion, they looked across the wild waters. In the moonlight, they could see that the whole section of high girders had disappeared. The train was nowhere to be seen.

Gradually, the full extent of the tragedy became known. The force of the gale had caught the train as it crossed the central section of the great bridge. The whole mass of girders, with the train inside, had crashed into the torrent below. Seventy-five people had plunged to their deaths.

The news of the disaster came as an enormous shock to Britain. It was hard for engineers and builders to believe that the world's largest bridge had collapsed. A full enquiry was held. And from all of the careful investigation, blame was pointed at one man in particular. This was Sir Thomas Bouch. His bridge had been badly designed, badly constructed and badly maintained. He had not allowed sufficient strength in the girders. Nuts and bolts had come loose. Trains had travelled too fast over the bridge. He was a broken man and died soon afterwards.

Railway building was an important part of Victorian life. But the Tay Bridge Disaster was remembered as a most heavy blow in the story of the progress. It was a reminder that even in an age of great engineers, the powers of nature were vast.

1882
The Phoenix Park Murders

TENSION ERUPTS IN IRELAND

Ghastly murder in Dublin: Lord Frederick Cavendish stabbed: Search for killers

Phoenix Park is in Dublin. On the early evening of 6th May 1882, two gentlemen were strolling through the grounds. They walked along a broad road which ran through the park, chatting as they went. It was a pleasant evening and various groups of people were moving about. As the two men moved through one of these groups, they were attacked suddenly and violently. One of the victims was stabbed savagely in the back with a long surgical knife. Then his throat was cut. The other victim turned to help his friend, but was struck. He fell and then received a stab wound under his armpit. Within a few moments, one man was dead and the other lay dying. The group of murderers jumped on to a jaunting-car – a type of horse-drawn carriage – which was waiting. They galloped off as fast as possible.

Some other people in the park had seen the squabble but it was not for some time that anyone realised that a murder had taken place. Then two cyclists came along and gave the alarm.

The news of the killings sent a shock of horror through England and Ireland. The victims were two men of the greatest importance in dealings between the two countries. Their deaths had deep results on relations between both lands for a number of years. One was Thomas Burke, the Under-Secretary for Ireland. The other was Lord Frederick Cavendish, the new Chief Secretary. He had left London only on the previous day to take up his appointment. What made the killing even more of a shock was that Cavendish was related to Gladstone, the English Prime Minister. He had married Gladstone's niece and had been specially chosen to carry out some vital work in Ireland.

The murderers had intended to attack Burke. He was an Irishman and an official of the Government. For many years he had helped to carry out the policy of the British Government. At that time, the whole of Ireland was part of Great Britain. Southern Ireland did not exist as a separate country, as it does today. Many Irishmen were angered by British policy. They were full of hatred for any Irishman who helped to carry it out.

All through the nineteenth century, Ireland remained a great problem to British governments. Many rich Englishmen owned estates there but did not take an interest in the welfare of their tenants. The Irish people wanted reform to be carried out. They wished to own the land which they tilled and they wished to govern themselves.

W. E. Gladstone devoted a great part of his political career to trying to solve the Irish Problem. In 1880 he became Prime Minister for the second time. He determined to make a great effort to cure the difficulties of Ireland. In recent years matters had grown very bad in that country. Some landlords had evicted their tenants. That means that they had put them out from the houses and land which they rented. Sometimes they did this in an effort to farm their land more efficiently. On other occasions they did it because the tenants had not paid rent. Often it led to great hardships when families were driven from their homes.

The Irish formed a Land League in 1879. Its members hoped to protect tenants and to gain

Irish peasants being evicted from their home

Home Rule for their country. In the following year, C. S. Parnell became its President. He was also the leader of the Irish members in the House of Commons. In Ireland, the Land League was severe on any Irishman who took over the land of an evicted man. Acts of violence were carried out on people who disobeyed the League's orders. In England, Parnell and his followers took every chance of causing trouble in Parliament. They kept debates going for hours and disturbed the business of the Commons.

In October 1881, Parnell was imprisoned. He had urged Irishmen to resist the English. A period of terror and violence followed in Ireland. Rents were not paid. Men were murdered. Many landlords had to be given police protection. Hundreds of families were evicted. By April 1882, Gladstone and Parnell came to an agreement. They saw the need for co-operation. The period of burning and bloodshed in Ireland had to be stopped. Therefore, on 2nd May Parnell was released from prison. It appeared that an age of new hope would begin. At the same time, Gladstone announced that he had chosen a new Lord Lieutenant and a new Chief Secretary for Ireland. The former position was to be filled by Lord Spencer. The latter was given to Lord Frederick Cavendish. They both left for Dublin, determined to carry out their duties as well as they could.

They did not know that a group of Irishmen had been plotting for some time. These men belonged to a secret society known as the Irish Invincibles. Their policy was to use force to gain freedom for their country. They had planned to kill the former Chief-Secretary, but had failed to make an attempt. The Under-Secretary, Thomas Burke, was to be their next victim. A group of the Invincibles lay in wait in Phoenix Park. They knew that

Lord Frederick Cavendish

Burke would pass by, going to his house. As the Under-Secretary made his way along, he met Lord Cavendish. Both men walked together, enjoying the evening stroll. One of the plotters who knew Burke gave the signal that he was approaching. Probably the Invincibles did not know who the other man was.

The murders caused an outcry in England and Ireland. Some people blamed Gladstone. They claimed that he was not tough enough towards the Irish. Many blamed Parnell, because they said that his policy had encouraged violence. A number of Irishmen were pleased that Burke had been killed. To them, the Invincibles were patriots whose crime was no greater than many others being carried out at that time.

At length, the men involved in the plot were caught. In order to save himself, one named Carey gave evidence against his friends. Five were hanged and others imprisoned. Carey was sent off to South Africa, but was recognised on board ship and shot dead by another Irishman.

The train of long, bitter struggles in Ireland continued. The murders in Phoenix Park were just another incident in a sad story, which has still not found a peaceful and satisfactory end.

1882
The Oval Test Match

DETERMINED AUSTRALIANS WIN THE DAY

Well done, Australians!: English cricketers defeated: Close match at the Oval

The time was just after midday. A murmur of excitement went round the ground. The spectators leaned forward to watch the players come on to the field. The eleven cricketers were the pride of England. It was felt that they were a superb team. The batting was strong right the way down the order. The bowlers were experienced and there was a good balance in the attack. The fielding was keen, with fast running and throwing.

Cricket had been a well known game in some parts of England since the mid-eighteenth century. By 1882 it was growing increasingly popular. In an age when many people were beginning to gain more leisure, they wished to watch skilled entertainment. Some players were professionals, while others, who came from comfortable backgrounds, were amateurs.

The crowd at once recognised some of the players in England's Eleven. There was the famous Dr W. G. Grace. His tall, well-built figure and large black beard made him out-

The match in progress

The victorious Australian team. Spofforth, 'The Demon' stands fourth from the left

standing. There was Hornby, the captain, Ulyett, the bowler and Steel, the all-rounder. A few minutes later, the opposing opening batsmen came out of the pavillion to take their places at the wicket. They were the Australians, Massie and Bannerman. They faced up to England's opening bowlers, Peate and Ulyett. Thus began one of the most famous Test matches in the history of cricket.

The day was Monday 28th August 1882. The match was being held on Surrey's ground at Kennington Oval. The Australians had played their first game in May. From that time on, they won match after match. English cricket had always been supreme, but here was a team which challenged hard and was often successful. They had four remarkably good bowlers who helped them to win a string of victories. The Australians, however, had lost a couple of matches and it was obvious that England's players had a good chance in the Test Match. Therefore there was a keen interest shown in the game by the hundreds of spectators who packed the ground.

The crowd soon had reason to be pleased with England's team. Australian wickets began to fall. By lunch, six were lost for only 48 runs. The game started again in the afternoon and England's success continued. The Australians were all out within twenty minutes and they had scored only 64 runs. That was the lowest total made in any of their matches. The English bowler, Barlow, took five wickets for 19 runs.

When England's innings opened, hopes were high that a big score would be made. It was expected that the Australian total would be passed easily. However, the English batsmen were soon in trouble. The Australian fast bowler, Spofforth, quickly took two wickets. One of them was that of the great W. G. Grace, one of the very best batsmen ever. He was bowled for only four runs. Gradually the English total climbed. The batsmen had to struggle hard for every run. By the time that the Australian total had been reached, six wickets had fallen. At length, 102 runs were made. By then the day's play was over.

During the night, there were heavy downpours which drenched the ground. Further rain next morning held up play for a little time. When it started, the wicket was 'dead' and the Australian opening batsmen took advantage of it. They launched an onslaught on the bowling. In less than an hour they put on 66 runs and Massie made 55 of them. The game first swung one way, then the other. The Australian captain, Murdoch, played well, but the bowlers had some success. When the innings finished, the visitors had made 122. This gave them a lead of 84.

The spectators carefully weighed up the chances. It should have been easy for the English team to score the 85 runs needed to win. They had so many good batsmen in the side. Yet the Australians had shown many times that they were very tough opponents. They did not give in easily and loved to fight back hard when in difficulties.

When England's innings began, the batsmen were made to struggle for every run. The Australian bowlers, Spofforth and Garrett gave nothing away. However, the total gradually crept up. When 50 had been scored, only

two wickets had fallen. The scales had swung England's way. But then the trouble started and the bowlers rose to great heights. At 53, the fourth wicket fell and that was the Champion's, 'W.G.' himself. He had scored 32 runs.

The battle grew very tense. At one stage, the Australians bowled twelve maiden overs in succession. Although the batsmen tried hard, wickets continued to fall. When 75 runs had been scored and only 10 were needed to win, there were still two wickets left. However, they produced only 2 more runs before Peate, England's last batsman was bowled.

The crowd had followed the innings with growing excitement. Fortunes had swung backwards and forwards. As the end came, they stood to cheer the winners. Spofforth was carried off like a hero. He was known as 'The Demon' and was the most feared of the Australian bowlers. In the last stages of the match, he had taken four wickets for 2 runs and had captured fourteen wickets in the whole match.

Many people in England were surprised that their team, which was usually known as 'The M.C.C.' – Marylebone Cricket Club – had been beaten. It seemed incredible that men could come from the other side of the world, to the home of cricket and defeat such fine players. The Australians, however, had shown the qualities that have always been associated with their cricket. They refused to give in and fought their way to victory.

A little later, a newspaper, the *Sporting Times*, published a notice. From that time, cricket matches between England and Australia were said to be for 'The Ashes'. The notice ran:

In Affectionate Remembrance

of

ENGLISH CRICKET

which died at the Oval

on

29th August, 1882

Deeply lamented by a large circle of

Sorrowing Friends and Acquaintances

R.I.P.

N.B. – The body will be cremated, and the Ashes taken to Australia

The Ashes trophy

1885
Gordon at Khartoum

GENERAL STRANDED – NO HELP CAME

Gordon killed at Khartoum: Relief came too late: Was Government too slow to help?

The Queen was upset and blamed Mr Gladstone, the Prime Minister, for not taking action. She felt that he had left a brave man in the lurch. A number of Conservative politicians agreed. They believed that the government had shown weakness. Some newspapers attacked the Prime Minister for not being strong and sending soldiers in time. Others supported him and pointed out that the brave man had not obeyed the government's orders. He had tried to do more than his instructions allowed.

The year was 1885 and news had just reached Britain of an event in Africa. There, at the city of Khartoum, General Charles Gordon had been killed. The city which he had been defending, was lost to the enemy. The British relief forces had arrived too late to save him. The event was a great tragedy.

Khartoum is the chief city of the Sudan. That large country lies to the south of Egypt. Britain became closely involved in the affairs of Egypt after buying the Suez Canal shares in 1875. Thus she also became involved in the Sudan. The Egyptians had held power in the Sudan for many years. They had treated it as part of their empire. But their government there was often weak and corrupt.

By the early 1880s, many people in the Sudan wished to overthrow Egyptian rule. In May 1881 a rebellion began. It was centred round a most remarkable man. A Moslem holy man named Mohammed Ahmed announced that he was a special prophet sent from God. The title given to such a prophet

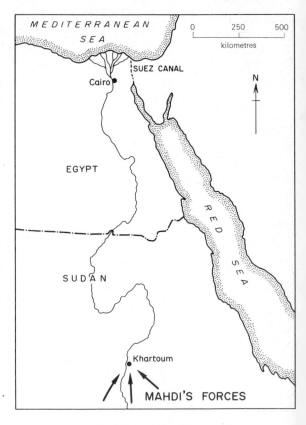

Egypt and the Sudan

was 'The Mahdi'. He had led a life of strict prayer and thought. Soon he gathered a group of followers round him.

The Mahdi's claim was sent to governors and tribal chiefs throughout the Sudan. At first, some accepted him, but others thought that he was a fraud. But when the Governor-General sent an armed force to arrest him, they were almost wiped out by the Mahdi's followers.

The soldiers of the Mahdi fought with fanatical courage. They did not fear death in battle because they believed that it would bring them a place in Heaven. The name given to them was Dervishes. Using these men, the Mahdi gradually conquered large areas of the Sudan. Anyone who did not accept his claim was attacked. Several forces of Egyptians were beaten.

After 1882, when British forces invaded Egypt, various British officers became closely involved in what was going on in the Sudan. They were worried that the Mahdi might invade Egypt. Therefore they believed that his armies should be brought to battle. Some retired British officers were employed by the Egyptians to serve in the Sudan. One was Colonel Hicks. In September 1883 he left Khartoum with a force of 10,000 Egyptian troops. They were attacked by the Mahdi's forces and massacred. Gradually, the religious leader's troops grew stronger. They began to advance towards Khartoum.

In Britain, a Liberal Government was in power. The Prime Minister was Mr Gladstone. He did not really want to interfere in the affairs of other countries. Many of his supporters wanted Britain to have nothing to do with Egypt and the Sudan. But others stated that the Mahdi should be stopped by British power. The Egyptians sought more and more help from Britain. At length, the British government decided to send an officer to the Sudan. His task would be to give a report on the situation there. He would take control of the garrison at Khartoum. Then he was to withdraw them northwards into Egypt.

In January 1884 they chose one of the most able, but unusual Englishmen who lived during the nineteenth century. He was General Charles Gordon. He was born in 1833, the son of a soldier. His lifetime had been spent in Army service. To the public he was known as 'Chinese' Gordon, because he had waged a successful campaign against Chinese rebels some years earlier. He knew the Sudan well because he had seen service there from 1874 to 1879. At that time he was employed by the Khedive of Egypt.

Gordon had gained a great reputation with the British people. They thought of him as a

General Gordon

fine officer who could manage foreigners easily. They knew that he had strong religious views. He was a most unusual character. Therefore it was widely felt that he would soon solve the problem in the Sudan.

But when Gordon arrived there he found that the situation was very difficult. The Mahdi's forces grew immensely strong. It became increasingly difficult to keep in touch with the outside world as the Dervishes drew closer to the city. However, Gordon did not evacuate Khartoum. He believed that the Mahdi could be defeated. Therefore he stayed. There is still argument over whether or not Gordon acted correctly. Some people say that he was guarding Britain's interests. Others

Gordon meets his death

say that he disobeyed orders.

He was not always an easy man to deal with. The British government feared that Gordon could involve them in trouble. Therefore, they sent no help for some time. But in Britain there was public pressure to send support. Newspapers printed articles which begged the government to do something. At last, by the end of September, 1884, a force of soldiers was made ready. They were under the command of Lord Wolseley, a famous soldier. Their journey was long and slow. They had a great amount of equipment to carry. Thus, they did not appear at Khartoum until 28th January 1885. But the Mahdi's forces had captured the city two days before.

For months, Gordon had led the defenders. They beat off many attacks. He organised the defences, with trenches, barbed wire and forts. Also, he had some armed steamers, which sailed on the Nile and attacked the enemy. However, the Dervishes were strong. In the early hours of 26th January, when the British relief force was quite near, they stormed into Khartoum. Gordon, dressed in a white uniform, met them. He stood on the steps of the Palace and faced his enemies. The British soldier was quite calm. With shouts, they leapt at him, stabbing with spears and swords. In a few moments he was dead.

When the news reached Britain, the great outcry followed. It was aimed at Gladstone and his government. The storm raged on for months. Yet afterwards, the question remained. Had Gordon been let down by the British government or had he gone further than his orders allowed?

1889
The Dockers' Strike

THE FIGHT FOR THE 'TANNER'

Dockers on strike: Sixpence an hour demanded: A long struggle ahead

A large group of working men stood at a street corner. They were listening to one of their number making a speech. He was standing on a box in a shop doorway. His audience followed every word with the utmost care. They were dockers and all were on strike. The speaker was urging them not to give in. He reminded them how important it was not to ease up in the fight. He said that they had right on their side. The men had been on strike for more than three weeks already. Now they grimly decided to carry on. The dockers were roughly dressed. From their appearance it was obvious that they were used to hard physical work. They were members of the lower working class and lived in an age when life was extremely hard for such people.

The month was September, 1889. The event is generally known as the Great Dock Strike or the strike for the 'Docker's Tanner'. It was one of the most important events in the story of trade unions in Britain. When the men stopped work, the whole port of London was

A procession of strikers

brought to a standstill. The events of the strike were remembered for years afterwards by those who had taken part.

At that time, dockers were among the worst paid workers in the land. They lived in conditions of poverty, often in slum areas which were close to the docks. The men had little steady work and had few chances of improving the conditions under which they worked. They were the lower paid employees who had no strong unions to represent them. During the nineteenth century, unions grew in power. Gradually, they came to gain higher wages and better working conditions for their members. But it was the skilled craftsmen who did best from such bargaining. Unskilled workers gained little.

Most dockers were casual labourers. In 1889 there were still many sailing ships. It was not easy to predict when they would arrive, because so much depended upon weather conditions. Therefore there could be a great deal of work for a short time, followed by a period of unemployment. Early each morning, hundreds of men would appear at the dock gates. There they would seek work. There was jostling, shouting and arguing as they tried to get employment for the day. Those who were lucky were taken on. The scores who were unlucky were faced with a day's idleness. Such a system caused great misery to many men and their families.

Numbers of men belonged to a small union. This was the Tea Operatives' and General Labourers' Association, founded by a warehouseman named Ben Tillett. Today, trade unions have strength and bargain freely with employers. However, at that time, they had been recognised as lawful for only a few years. There was no well organised power behind them to support their efforts.

Tillett wished to improve the men's con-

An early forerunner of Trade Unionism: A membership card of the
International Working Men's Association of 1869

ditions. Therefore, on 7th August 1889 one of the dock employers was asked to pay higher wages to his men. The wage had been 5 pence an hour, with 7 pence an hour for overtime. He was asked to raise these figures to 6 pence and 8 pence respectively. After he had consulted other employers, he refused. Immediately, casual labourers at the East India and West India docks stopped work. The strike had begun. $[6d = 2\frac{1}{2}p]$

At once, the strikers found forceful helpers. One was Tom Mann, who helped with the organisation. Another was John Burns, a former ship's engineer. Burns believed that the dockers had a just cause in asking for more pay. He was determined to lead the men to victory.

The employers believed that the strike would not last for long. They knew that the men had little money to support them. There was no National Assistance from the State in those days. Therefore the dockers would soon face starvation. They would be forced to give in. Some men refused to strike. Burns and Tillett realised that these had to be stopped. Otherwise, work at the docks would not be brought to a standstill. Therefore pickets were organised. These were groups of strikers who stood at the dock gates and tried to stop men entering or leaving. They were paid 2 shillings (10p) a day for their work. Sometimes they used violence. Fists flew as small crowds clashed in the streets.

Burns wanted publicity for his cause. He organised processions of dockers. They walked through the streets of London, going towards the West End. Carrying banners and singing, they hoped to draw attention to their cause. The leaders hoped that the public would show sympathy. One form of help was needed every day and that was money. Therefore collecting tins were taken round.

Matters became very difficult for the dockers' families. They had never had much in life, but now things were very hard. However, the strike committee made great efforts to help those in real need. Food and money were provided. As the strike went on, support came from many places. The Lord Mayor of London started a fund which raised nearly

The strike committee at work

£1,500. On the other side of the World, Australian workers made collections of more than £25,000. The Salvation Army provided food.

The daily march through London grew larger and larger. It was often like a carnival. Bands played, banners were waved and strikers cheered, jeered, sang and shouted. On 16th August, 60,000 people took part. Twelve days later, there were 90,000 marchers. Gradually, pressure was put on the employers to grant the 'Dockers' Tanner'. That was their claim for sixpence an hour ($2\frac{1}{2}$p). The Lord Mayor set up a committee of well known men to solve the problem of the strike. It included the famous Roman Catholic, Cardinal Manning.

At length, the employers gave way. They agreed to the improvements which had been asked for by Tillett and Burns. There was an amount of fighting when the men went back to work on 16th September. There were fights between those who had been on strike and those who had refused. However, the dockers had won a great and remarkable victory. Unskilled workers in industry realised that they need not be badly treated. They saw the value of making a united stand. The Dock Strike of 1889 was an important event in the history of trade unions, occurring at a time when these organisations were growing in influence and power.

1896
London to Brighton

FOURTEEN CARS COMPLETE THE RUN

Red Flag Act repealed: Motorists celebrate: Cars driven from London to Brighton

The villagers at the roadside stared. None of them had ever seen such a vehicle before. They had heard about them but this was the first one to pass through their part of Sussex. It was an early motor car which chugged its way up the hill. There were two occupants. One was the driver who leant forward over the small steering wheel. The other was one of his friends who had come along to help him on the journey. The men were dressed very differently from motorists of the present day. Each wore a heavy leather coat, with a scarf wrapped several times round the neck. On their heads they had caps which were well pulled down. Their eyes were protected by goggles.

With a spluttering engine the car made slower progress as the hill became steeper. At length it stopped, with smoke and steam pouring out from underneath. Some of the villagers ran forward to push. After some heaving and straining, the vehicle managed to reach the top. The driver gave a wave of thanks then his car clattered away down into the next valley.

The date was 14th November 1896. Although most of the watchers did not realise it at the time, they were witnessing a most important event. The event was of the greatest importance in the story of Britain's transport. That day is still celebrated each year. At the time, it did not make headline news in newspapers. Nevertheless, the pioneers were so pleased that the issue of the magazine *Autocar* was printed in red ink.

Early motor cars were built in Europe. Towards the end of the nineteenth century, many scientists and engineers became aware of the value of the petrol engine. Experiments were carried out, especially in Germany and France. They aimed to produce a light, powerful engine and then to mount it in a small vehicle. Thus there could be a 'horseless carriage'.

Two Germans have become famous for introducing this new form of transport. It soon brought vast changes to a society which had used the horse for road travel during many centuries. Their names were Carl Benz and Gottlieb Daimler. They did not work together, yet each one produced a successful vehicle. In 1885, Benz built a motor tricycle and soon began selling similar models. Daimler, in the same year fitted a petrol engine on to a type of motor cycle. In the next year, he produced a carriage powered by an engine.

The French began a car building industry. Machines were made and sold freely, although only well-to-do people could buy them. The motorists were able to drive about freely, with few restrictions.

But the new form of transport was not successful in Britain. Although some of the cars were imported from across the Channel, one law stood in their way. This was the 'Locomotives on Highways Act (1865)', better known as 'The Red Flag Act'. The measure had been passed especially to stop the development of steam vehicles on British roads. Those people who were connected with railways or with horse-drawn road transport were very pleased when the Act was passed. It laid down that any vehicle, not drawn by animals, which went on a road, had to have three

Old and New in the Early Days

persons to work it. One of them had to walk at least 60 metres in front. By day he had to carry a red flag, or by night a red lamp. Thus people would be warned of the approaching vehicle. Its speed limit was laid down as 4 mph (6·4 k.p.h.) in the country and only 2 mph (3·2 k.p.h.) in towns.

The roads of Britain were not the country's most important transport links during the Victorian Age. It was the railway which had become vital. The country was covered by a network of lines. People and goods were transported at speeds of up to 75 mph (120 k.p.h.) between towns, cities and villages. The coming of the railway had brought disaster to many coaching companies. Inns and stables had fallen into disuse.

However, with the coming of the motor car, some men could foresee its usefulness. It was a small form of personal transport. Those rich enough to buy a car would find the vehicle convenient. Therefore pressure was brought in Parliament to have the law changed.

Several members spoke out strongly about the advantages of cars. They mentioned that the Prince of Wales himself had visited an exhibition of cars which had been held at South Kensington. But there were strong forces opposed to them. Many people believed that motors were dirty and noisy. However, on 14th November 1896 the 'Red Flag Act' was changed. It was no longer necessary to have a man walking in front of the car. Also, the speed limit was raised – to 12 mph (19·2 k.p.h.).

In celebration, a number of motorists decided to drive from London to Brighton. Altogether, thirty-three cars were entered for the run. Their route passed down through Surrey, into Sussex. Some cars were brought over from the Continent to take part. Gottlieb Daimler came over to make the drive. The journey proved to be very difficult for many of those taking part. There were not the good roads, with garages which exist today. When there were small faults in the engines, the

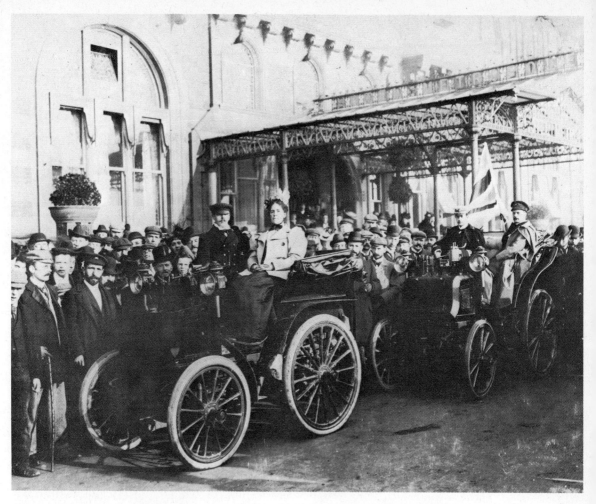

The start of the first London to Brighton run in 1896

drivers themselves had to mend them. As the day went on, the weather grew bad. Sometimes, passengers had to get out and push. At the end, some fourteen cars only managed to complete the journey. Nevertheless, a new chapter of British motoring had opened.

British car production started later than that in Germany and France. However, over the following years it was built up in such places as Coventry and Birmingham. Herbert Austin and Frederick Lanchester soon became well known as motor engineers. By the end of the nineteenth century the motor car had just made its appearance on Britain's roads. Before long it was to become of great importance in daily life for many people.

1898
The Death of Gladstone

AN ENGLISH STATESMAN DIES

Grand Old Man passes on: End of Mr Gladstone's long life: A great politician

Throughout Britain's history, some famous politicians have emerged. Their lives and work have affected many of their fellow countrymen. From time to time, a few of these politicians have shown signs of real greatness. They have stood out above others in what they achieved. They have become well known and respected in their own lifetimes.

One of these men died on 19th May 1898. He was William Ewart Gladstone. His death brought to an end links with politics which went back to the first half of the nineteenth century. Thousands of people in Britain and her Empire mourned the passing of a great statesman.

Gladstone was born in Liverpool in 1809. He came from a well-to-do family who lived in comfort. As a boy, he was sent to Eton, the public school. Later, he entered Oxford University. There he showed himself to be a superb scholar. He learned Latin and Greek and began to master the writing and speaking of the English language. The young man was deeply religious. At one time he hoped to enter the Church. However, he felt that he would be able to serve God by a life in politics.

Therefore in 1833 he stood for election. He chose the Tory Party, from which the Conservative Party of the present day has developed. He was elected as a member for the town of Newark. During his early years in Parliament, Gladstone was a stern Tory. He was opposed to many of the reforms which were carried out in the 1830s. Before long he attracted attention because he was a fine speaker. Sir Robert Peel, the Prime Minister offered him various posts in the government. Gladstone showed great ability, especially in matters concerned with finance and trade.

In 1846 the Tory Party was split over the repeal of the Corn Laws. Most Tories broke away from Peel, but Gladstone and a few others remained loyal. Later, in 1852, he accepted a place in a government formed by Lord Aberdeen, a Whig. The old Whig Party

William Ewart Gladstone

later developed into the Liberal Party. Gladstone served as Chancellor of the Exchequer and proved himself to be a brilliant finance minister. He tried to introduce many of the ideas of Free Trade.

During the later 1850s he would not belong to either party. Gladstone did not like either Disraeli, the Tory leader or Palmerston, who led the Whigs. In spite of this he was a man of such great ability that the country needed his services. Therefore in 1859 he again became Chancellor in a Whig government. He remained in that position until 1865. Through his policies, Britain's trade expanded. Taxes were low. There was an income tax but it dropped to 4 pence (2p) in the £1!

Soon after this, Gladstone became leader of the Whig Party. By then he was well known as a politician. At a General Election in 1868, the Liberals won. Therefore he became Prime Minister for the first time. Over the next six years the government carried out many measures of reform in Britain. The Liberals had to deal with such matters as Irish troubles, education and army reform.

By 1874 they had achieved a great deal. However, many Britishers felt that Gladstone was weak in dealing with other nations. His party was defeated at the General Election. He announced that he was retiring from political life. Gladstone was happily married. His wife was a great help to him in his work. They owned a large estate at Hawarden, in North Wales. There he was able to pass happy hours, often carrying out his favourite relaxation of felling trees.

He was a wonderful public speaker. Vast crowds gathered to listen and watch when he made a large speech. The fine head, the piercing eyes and the powerful voice made him a very grand figure. Gladstone was strict and severe. He tried to remind people of their duty towards others. He was very religious and appealed to Britishers to help those in life who were not so fortunate.

However, he was not liked by Queen Victoria. Although he stood for many things that were right in public life, she was never on good terms with him. Gladstone was not at ease with her. She felt that he was boring and full

of his own importance. She claimed that the Liberal leader often spoke to her as he would address a public meeting. The Queen much preferred his great rival, Disraeli, for whom she had a great liking.

Gladstone re-entered political life in 1876 when he attacked Disraeli's policy towards Turkey. Three years later, he went back to Parliament as MP for Midlothian, in Scotland. His election campaign was one of the most famous events in his life. Then in 1880 the Liberals won a General Election. Once more, Gladstone became Prime Minister.

During this period of Liberal rule, there were many troubles. Gladstone was realising that Home Rule was needed in Ireland. However, many other English politicians did not agree with him. Difficulties continued in that country. Egypt and the Sudan also presented problems. These ended with General Gordon being besieged and killed at Khartoum in 1885. Gladstone was widely blamed for letting him die.

'The Grand Old Man'

The Gladstone family in later years

For the rest of his political life, the Liberal leader was mainly concerned with the problem of Ireland. In 1886 he introduced his first Home Rule Bill. He was magnificent in debate. Carefully and clearly he pointed out the justice of his ideas. But the questions of land and religion were very difficult. Many of his own party disagreed with him. The Liberals lost the election and were out of power for six years.

Gladstone showed enormous strength, although he was an old man. He travelled round the country, addressing public meetings. In the House of Commons he took an active part in debates. In 1892 he once again became Prime Minister. At the age of eighty-two, he made another attempt to solve the Irish problem. He introduced a second Home Rule Bill, but it failed. Therefore, early in 1894, the famous man left office. He was known as 'The Grand Old Man' of British politics. His last few years were spent peacefully at Hawarden. Gladstone's death marked the end of an age in political life.

1899
Black Week

DEFEAT FOLLOWS DEFEAT

Britain's Black Week: Three defeats by Boers: Farmers fight skilfully

The news was very bad. A short time before, it appeared that the British Army were about to win a campaign. They looked set to win comfortably, and thus end the war quickly. Their opponents did not have the supplies of men, money or munitions that the British forces had. The enemy were mainly farmers, not fitted to fight a war against a well equipped army.

Yet as the news came in and the newspapers prepared their headlines, it appeared that defeats had been suffered. In one week the British Army had received three major setbacks. This is why people discussed the events with grave faces and heavy hearts. The week was soon known as Black Week.

The month was December 1899 and the nineteenth century was drawing to a close. In those days, Britain was an extremely powerful nation. She possessed the largest empire ever known in the history of the modern world. Her territories were to be found in all parts of the globe. The Royal Navy was the strongest force of warships in existence. The combined wealth and strength gave Britain her supreme position. Thus the news of British defeats came as a surprise to the nation.

The troubles had occurred several thousand kilometres away, in South Africa. The war was being fought there against the Boers. Ever since the seventeenth century, there had been settlers of Dutch descent at the southern tip of Africa. They had a language and a way of life of their own. Most of them were farmers.

Britain had become interested in that part of the world from the time of the Napoleonic Wars. Then, British forces occupied the Cape of Good Hope. After 1815, it became part of the Empire. The Cape became an important stopping point on the way to the Far East. From that period, relations between the Boers and the British were often poor. There were several outbreaks of trouble during the nineteenth century. In 1881, a short war occurred. Over the last twenty or thirty years of the century the 'Scramble for Africa' took place. This was a rush by European countries to gain colonies in The Dark Continent. Germany, Belgium and Italy are examples of the states which sought territories there. But the country which played the greatest part

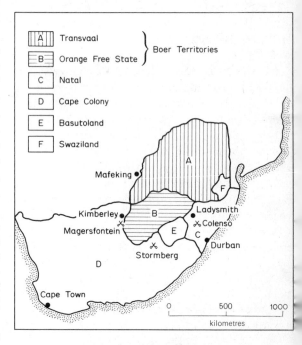

The area of trouble

Grenadier Guards pinned down at Modder River

was Britain. She did not do so willingly, but she was determined that other lands should not gain advantages over her. Vast areas of Africa were taken over as part of the British Empire. The policy is often called Imperialism.

This policy worried the Boers. They feared that the British were trying to take their land. They believed that they might lose their freedom and be taken into Britain's Empire. This was a threat they were determined to resist. By the end of the century, there were four major territories in South Africa. Two were Boer republics – Transvaal and the Orange Free State. Cape Colony and Natal were British.

The Prime Minister of Cape Colony was Cecil Rhodes. He hoped that British lands in Africa would stretch 'from Cairo to the Cape'. One of his great ambitions was to see the map of Africa 'painted red'. It was not long before this policy came into conflict with the Boers. Rhodes encouraged some Britishers who lived in the Transvaal to rebel against the Government there. They had fewer rights than the Boers. Part of the attempt in 1895, known as the Jameson Raid, failed dismally. Rhodes had to resign.

The Boers started to buy arms, especially from Germany. They were filled with a distrust of Britain. They bought field guns, Maxim guns and rifles. Extra British forces were sent to Natal.

President Paul Kruger was leader of the Boers. He demanded that these forces should be withdrawn. Britain refused to agree. Therefore in October 1899 the Boers declared war on the greatest empire in the world. David had attacked Goliath!

At the beginning of the war, British forces in South Africa were rather weak. The Boers soon showed themselves to be excellent fighters. They were horsemen, armed with rifles. Most were expert shots. They knew the country well and were very mobile. Forces of the British Army tried to fight the war in an old fashioned way. Most of them were foot soldiers. They moved slowly and made targets for Boer riflemen.

Soon there were setbacks. The Boers attacked in several places. They advanced swiftly and easily. Before long they besieged forces in three places. These were Ladysmith, Mafeking and Kimberley. In all three, the defending forces held out strongly.

Part of the Boer contingent at Ladysmith – The Boers proved to be clever soldiers and marksmen

In November an army corps arrived from Britain. They came by sea and consisted of thousands of men, horses, wagons and guns. The Commander was General Sir Redvers Buller. There was no doubt about his personal bravery. As a younger soldier, he had twice won the Victoria Cross. But he had never before fought a campaign like the one he now met. One of his first aims was to relieve Kimberley and Ladysmith. He decided to attack the enemy as soon as possible. His Army Corps was split into three parts. Early in December 1899 each one went into action.

General Sir William Gatacre led a force of 3,000 men against the Boers near a place called Stormberg. His opponents had placed their forces carefully along a range of hills known as the Kissieberg. The British were badly led. They blundered into heavy fire and were forced to retreat. More than 600 surrendered. It was the first defeat of 'Black Week'.

Another force, under Lord Methuen, consisted of 13,000 men. They marched to relieve Kimberley. In front lay the Magersfontein Hills, which the Boers had carefully defended with trenches. British troops ran into a withering fire. Immense bravery was shown by both sides. However, Methuen was forced to retreat after suffering more than a thousand casualties. That was the second defeat of the week.

On the following day Buller himself set out with 18,000 troops to relieve Ladysmith. At the village of Colenso, the Boers had carefully hidden themselves. Once again, the enemy fire was heavy and accurate. Buller lost more than 1,100 men and ten field guns. He retreated, sending a message to the besieged garrison at Ladysmith. It advised them to surrender.

Thus the century ended with three great shocks. Seldom has so much bad news come so quickly to Britain. Her people knew that they had a hard war ahead.